C000058919

ABERDEEN IN 100 DATES

ELMA McMENEMY

The History Press

For Brian
with love and thanks for your sense of humour, eye for detail
and for giving me the time to complete this.

In memory of my godson,
Simon Marshall (1971–2014)
who loved all sorts of trivia.

First published 2016

The History Press
The Mill, Brimscombe Port
Stroud, Gloucestershire, GL5 2QG
www.thehistorypress.co.uk

British Library Cataloguing in Publication Data.
A catalogue record for this book is available from the British Library.

ISBN 978 0 7509 6031 1

Typesetting and origination by The History Press
Printed in Great Britain

Contents

Acknowledgements

I should like to thank the following for the help and support they have given me in researching and writing *Aberdeen in 100 Dates*:

Martin Hall and Barry Robertson of Aberdeen City and Aberdeenshire Archives; Dr Christopher P. Croly, Aberdeen City Historian; staff of Aberdeen City Libraries Local Studies Department; Aberdeen Harbour Board Management Team; Fiona Musk, NHS Grampian Archivist; the Friends of Stonehaven Open Air Pool; Hilary Hinton, Honorary Librarian, Medico-Chirugical Society; Ruth Duncan, Curator, The Gordon Highlanders' Museum; David N. Parkinson, Late Convener The Seven Incorporated Trades of Aberdeen; Kevin Brown, The Shore Porters' Society; Paul Higson, the North East Scotland Preservation Trust; Caroline Mitchell and Yvonne Thackery, Chivas Brothers; Andrew MacGregor, University of Aberdeen Library, Special Collections and Museums; Jonathan Shackleton, The Robert Gordon University; Royal Aberdeen Golf Club; The Commonwealth Games Federation; Jeff Lawrence of Holyoke, Massachusetts; Bev Clarke of Tasmania; Brian Lockhart, author of *Robert Gordon's Legacy*; Rebecca Abrams, author of *Touching Distance*; Blue Badge Guide Colleagues Pam Wells, Malcolm Milne and Lesley Miller (retired); Lorna Numbers and, not least, my husband, Brian McMenemy for his patience, constructive criticism and red-pen corrections.

Any mistakes are, of course, my own.

Introduction

The area in and around Aberdeen has been inhabited for at least 10,000 years. The evidence is still here to see – burial cairns, recumbent stone circles, hill forts and carved Pictish stones. A recent excavation, 15 miles west of the city, revealed what is believed to be the earliest calendar in the world, created more than 10,000 years ago. With no exact dates known, this early history is impossible to include within *Aberdeen in 100 Dates*. Similarly, the exact days are not known for the battle of *Mons Graupius* when the Romans routed the native Picts, nor for when the Vikings visited the city they considered a holiday resort and a place to trade.

Aberdeen was originally two separate and very different burghs. The first was founded by St Machar on the south bank of the River Don. This religious settlement became known as Old Aberdeen. Later a cathedral was built here and the first university was founded nearby. Meanwhile, an important harbour developed 2 miles south, at the estuary of the River Dee. These two settlements were linked from early times: originally the income from ships using the harbour was paid to the Bishops of Old Aberdeen. The thriving commercial town which grew up near the port had its own Mither Kirk, the Kirk of St Nicholas, which was the spiritual heart of what became New Aberdeen. Today, the church's medieval artefacts give an interesting insight into life at that time. It is the church where new councils are 'kirked' and significant memorial services are held. Many of the people mentioned in the pages which follow are buried in its ancient kirkyard.

In 1891 Old and New Aberdeen were amalgamated and Torry, formerly part of Kincardineshire, became part of the city. Other settlements were already integrated in Aberdeen as they were within the 'gas limits', that is, their piped gas supply was provided by the city system. Several outlying villages, including Dyce, Kingswells, Cults and Peterculter (pronounced 'petercooter'), are now also incorporated in Aberdeen. The city has had a long association with its hinterland. Buchan and Mar were part of the Sheriffdom of Aberdeen as early as 1136 and the city's history is inextricably linked with that of the old counties which now comprise Aberdeenshire. Therefore some events from outside the city itself have been included in this book.

Aberdeen's development as the city we know today has been influenced by academic institutions, commerce and industries which changed over the centuries: textiles, fishing, agriculture, papermaking, granite, shipbuilding, whaling, tourism and offshore oil and gas. The 100 dates have been chosen to reflect as many of these as possible and to give a feeling for life in the city from the earliest times to the present day.

Much information for these 100 dates has come, directly or indirectly, from Aberdeen's amazing burgh records, held by Aberdeen City and Aberdeenshire Archives. The burgh registers from 1398–1509 have been recognised by UNESCO's Memory of the World Programme.

Elma McMenemy,
May 2016

ABERDEEN
IN 100 DATES

Whit Sunday

Machar, or Mocumma, is believed to have arrived on this day on the island of Iona. He was one of twelve disciples who accompanied St Columba on his voyage from Ireland. The *Aberdeen Breviary*, published 1,000 years after he lived, tells how St Machar brought Christianity to the Don Valley and Aberdeen.

St Columba sent Machar to travel east across the Scottish mainland and spread the word of God to the Picts. Machar's mission was to find a river which flowed in the shape of a bishop's pastoral staff. He found this place near the estuary of the River Don and built a small church in the area we now know as Old Aberdeen. West of Aberdeen in Strathdon are 'Macker's Haugh' and *Tobar Mhachar*, Machar's Well, a spring which miraculously provided fine salmon at a time of famine.

The Cathedral Church of St Machar now stands on the site of Machar's church. Inside, a granite stone, carved with a primitive cross, is displayed. This has been scientifically dated to the time of St Machar and is believed to be from his church. The cathedral bearing his name is one of the world's oldest granite cathedrals. Most of the present building dates from the 1300s and early 1400s. The magnificent heraldic ceiling was installed in 1520.

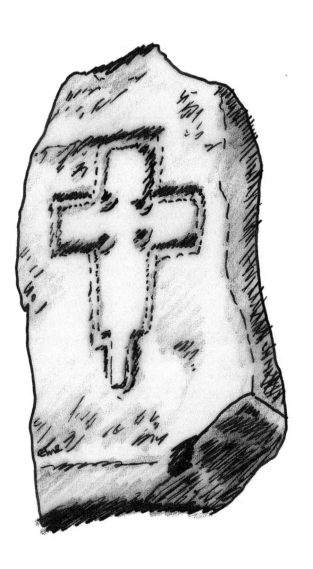

8 January

St Nathalan, also known as Nachlan, lived to a great age and died on this day. In modern times, his feast day is celebrated on 19 January. He is believed to have been born of a noble Pictish family at Tullich by the River Dee and is credited with many miracles. It is said that he gave away all his corn during a famine and, having no seed to sow, he scattered sand on his land and amazingly reaped a plentiful harvest. However, in another season Nathalan's crops failed and in frustration he blamed God. Filled with remorse for his outburst, he made a pilgrimage to Rome with his right arm chained and padlocked to his right leg as a penance. Before setting off he threw the key to the padlock into the River Dee. Months later, on arrival in Rome, he bought a fish to eat and on cutting it open he discovered the key to his padlock. Nathalan recognised this as a sign that God had forgiven him and released his chain. The Pope also acknowledged this miracle by making him a bishop.

Bishop Nathalan returned to Deeside where he built several churches. One of these was at Tullich. The ruins of a later church, built in the 1400s, now stand on the site of Nathalan's early church.

30 June

The small harbour at the estuary of the River Dee was already well used by this day, when King David I granted Bishop Nechtan of Aberdeen the right to the income from vessels using the anchorage and its facilities. This is accepted as the foundation date of Aberdeen Harbour Board, acknowledged as the UK's oldest business still in existence. At this time, vessels would anchor at the river mouth, sheltered on the north by Sandness, a large sandy promontory, and by high cliffs to the south. Small boats would ply back and forth, discharging the anchored ships' cargoes, delivering goods for export and ferrying the crews to and fro. Over the centuries, Aberdeen Harbour witnessed witches being 'tried' by douping from the Shorehead, pirates, who included prominent Aberdonians, shipwrecks and sailors quarantined on arrival from plague-infested ports. The harbour gradually developed during this time to become the successful modern port that today supports the oil and gas, and other, industries.

This early charter by King David also granted the bishops of Aberdeen other privileges, properties and lands, including half of the fisheries of the River Don. Many of these property and land rights were reaffirmed in the solemn privilege of Pope Adrian IV issued in 1157 for Bishop Edward of Aberdeen.

28 August

This is the date of the first charter granted to Aberdeen by King William I, known as William the Lion after he adopted the lion rampant as his coat of arms. The charter confirmed the rights given by his grandfather, David I, to the burgesses of Aberdeen. Burgesses were responsible citizens appointed as freemen and charged with guarding the burgh, its laws and customs. This charter, written in Latin, still exists in the city's archives and is the oldest of any Scottish burgh. It granted the burgesses the right to a free 'Hanse' or economic league, protected by the king, who forbade anyone to trouble or disturb them in their trade. At this time, charters were dated only with the day and month; the practice of showing a year was not adopted until the reign of William's son, Alexander II. However, 1179 is accepted as the most likely year, as the witnesses listed are known to have been present that year in Perth, where the charter was granted.

Aberdeen's burgesses were honoured again during William's reign when he visited their burgh, probably in 1201. They had contributed to the ransom paid for his freedom following his defeat and capture by Henry II of England. In gratitude, King William declared they need never pay any toll on their own goods 'wherever they come within my kingdom'.

24 October

Aberdeen's burgesses and citizens were rewarded for their loyal support of King Robert the Bruce on this day. Local legend tells that, around 1308, with its castle in the possession of the English, Aberdeen's citizens rose up and took it back in the name of the king. Their password was the French *Bon Accord*, meaning good agreement. Although there is no evidence to prove this story, the Royal Charter of 1313 is definitely a matter of record. In it, Robert I granted custodianship of his royal forest of Stocket to Aberdeen. This was royal hunting forest with open woodland that allowed good sport in hunting deer, wild boar and other game.

The Great Charter of 1319 granted more privileges to the burgesses and community of Aberdeen, including ownership of the burgh itself and the power to develop land within the forest of Stocket where they could 'perform every kind of tillage', erect dwelling houses and other buildings, dig fuel and much more. The burgh was also now granted the right to retain taxes raised from its citizens. This ensured a prosperous future for Aberdeen and laid the foundations of the burgh's Common Good Fund, still in existence today. Land purchased in the late 1300s and early 1400s, added to the Stocket forest, formed the basis of The Freedom Lands, their boundaries marked by March Stones.

24 July

Dawn on this day found Provost Davidson of Aberdeen and the Earl of Mar at the head of an army and striking camp at the confluence of the rivers Don and Urie. Together with many of Aberdeen's most influential citizens, they had marched out from the burgh to meet an invasion led by Donald, Lord of the Isles. This well-educated nobleman laid claim to the extensive Earldom of Ross, owned by the Earl of Mar. With an army of around 10,000 men, Donald had marched from the Highlands to seize this land. They were camped on a plateau near the 'fermtoun' of Harlaw, near Inverurie.

The Earl of Mar's force crossed the Urie and marched to Harlaw, where battle was joined. Despite an initial organised approach with formations of spearsmen, the fighting quickly degenerated into hand-to-hand combat. By sunset, Harlaw plateau was saturated, its streams running red with blood. The Lord of the Isles lost 900 Highlanders and 600 of the earl's men lay dead, among them Provost Davidson. Both sides claimed victory, but Donald retreated back to the Isles, his claim to the land unsuccessful.

A monument stands on the edge of the battlefield, now cultivated farmland. Built by Aberdeen City Council to commemorate the 500th anniversary of the battle, it honours the dead of both sides, featuring shields of the leaders, lairds and combatants who fought on this day.

22 January

Justice finally caught up with Sir Andrew Leslie of Balquhain (pronounced 'Balwhain') on this day when he was hunted down and killed by the Sheriff of Angus.

Nine years previously, the Leslies had fought bravely for the Earl of Mar at the Battle of Harlaw. It is not known exactly how many sons Sir Andrew lost on the battlefield as many of them were illegitimate. It was said that the baron had seventy children but most of them were 'unlawfully begotten'. Indeed, he was reputed to have fathered seven children in one night and 'all their Mothers lay in Child Bed at One Time'. His long-suffering lady sent food and money to each of these mothers to help support them and their babies. No woman or girl was safe from his attention and he is known to have carried off several 'fair maids', alienating his neighbours and many powerful families. Eventually the Sheriff of Angus was sent to put an end to the lascivious baron's activities. The sheriff and his men traced him to Braco, almost in the shadow of Bennachie near Inverurie and Harlaw. Here, Sir Andrew fought back and was killed. Although he was not buried where he fell, his widow arranged for a chapel to be built there. She also paid a priest to say Mass in the chapel every day for the repose of his soul.

6 February

At the burgh council meeting on this day, a list of 'baxtars' or bakers, together with their unique stamps or marks, was compiled and included in the minutes. At this time, each baker imprinted his loaves with his own mark. Should there be any query about the quality, size or weight of any bread, the mark could be used to trace the loaf back to an individual baker. If a baker were found to have sold a smaller, lighter loaf or to have used inferior flour, he would be punished. At this time, floor sweepings or even sawdust might be added to flour, so traceability was vital to ensure high standards. In 1442 the council had recorded that a penny loaf had to weigh at least 24oz after it had been baked.

This detailed list, with drawings representing the bakers' stamps, was the result of a long-running power struggle between the council and the bakers' trade. Since the early 1300s, the Burgh Court had determined the price of bread. A dispute between bakers over the price of loaves had resulted in a duel. One baker was killed while the other was fined 5*s* by the court. Although the bakers objected to the council regulating trade, eventually they became respected citizens and a few also became the burgh's provosts, as mayors are called in Scotland.

10 February

William Elphinstone, Bishop of Aberdeen, petitioned the Pope to found a university in Old Aberdeen and Pope Alexander VI granted a licence for the university's foundation, dated 10 February 1494. In the Middle Ages, New Year fell on the Feast of the Annunciation, 25 March; the document was therefore signed in the year now recognised as 1495.

The university, the third to be founded in Scotland and fifth in the UK, was named King's College to acknowledge the whole-hearted support of King James IV, a devout and learned man. This new university was founded to educate doctors, teachers and clergy for northern Scotland and lawyers and administrators for the Scottish Crown. Elphinstone brought Scottish-born Hector Boece from Paris to be the first principal. Arts, theology, canon and civil law were taught, initially with thirty-six staff and students based at St Machar's Cathedral. A Chair of Medicine was created in 1497, the first in the English-speaking world.

In 1500 work began on the university's first building, the chapel which features a crown tower. It was constructed on a raft of oak trunks to prevent it from sinking into the boggy ground. King's College Chapel is today interdenominational and very much still at the heart of the university. An elaborate monument, created in Venice in the early 1900s to commemorate Bishop Elphinstone, now stands outside the chapel.

21 April

In 1495 many Scottish soldiers were fighting for the French in Italy. When they returned they brought with them a newly discovered disease, known as the great pox to distinguish it from smallpox. It was almost certainly an early form of syphilis. Its primary symptoms included blue, black or white ulcers on the skin of the genitals. As the disease progressed, sores and pustules broke out over the whole body, tissue died in fingers, toes and other extremities and painful tumours developed before death occurred.

Aberdeen at this time had no burgh physician and no one yet appointed to the new Chair of Medicine. Despite this, the burgh's astute burgesses took prompt, preventative action. On this day they decreed: 'For the avoidance of the infirmity come out of France and strange parts ... all light women be charged and ordained to decist from their vices and sin of venery.' These 'light women', or prostitutes, were required to find lawful employment. If they failed to do so, they were to be punished by being branded and banished from the burgh. Aberdeen was the first authority anywhere in the United Kingdom to take any such measures to prevent the spread of disease.

22 June

Over 500 years ago 'pynours' or porters transported goods up the steep hill from Aberdeen Harbour to the market place, where the Castlegate and Mercat Cross stand today. On this day the pynours founded what was to become one of the earliest of all co-operative partnerships. Initially this was to protect their own interests. Later a property and warehousing department was set up. The income from this, called the Superannuated Members' Fund, was held completely separate from that of their day-to-day haulage business. It provided for members' retirement and was used to give financial support to any who were ill or injured.

This was the foundation of the Shore Porters' Society, now acknowledged as the world's oldest transport business. It is still a private partnership which operates successfully from headquarters close to Aberdeen Harbour and has expanded beyond north-east Scotland with a base and storage facilities in south-east England. From those early beginnings hauling goods within Aberdeen, imported from all over the world, the Shore Porters now transport to all parts of the globe. One of their more unusual deliveries was a consignment of sledges to Arctic Norway. Their warehouses store a wide range of commercial articles and personal property, from valuable antiques and works of art to wood. They also carry out commercial and house removals, or 'flittings' as they are better known in Aberdeen.

25 October

Bishop William Elphinstone, founder of King's College and guardian of the infant King James V, died on this day. Born in 1431, William Elphinstone spent his early life among the clergy of Glasgow Cathedral and University with his father, a churchman and first Dean of Arts of the university. He studied at universites in both Glasgow and Paris. In 1488 he was consecrated Bishop of Aberdeen and created Chancellor of Scotland by James III, who was killed in battle in the same year.

Bishop Elphinstone had a profound and far-reaching influence both in Aberdeen and throughout Scotland. An excellent statesman, diplomat, lawmaker and devout churchman, he travelled widely in Europe as the King's Ambassador. In Aberdeen, he founded King's College and continued the construction of St Machar's Cathedral, completing the great central tower with a spire and installing heavy bronze bells. He also instigated work for a stone bridge to form a safe crossing of the River Dee; on his death he bequeathed £20,000 to ensure the bridge was completed. In 1509 he brought the first printing press to Scotland and directed the production of Scotland's first printed book. Published in 1510, this was the Aberdeen Breviary, which contained prayers and writings about the lives of Scotland's saints. It is a treasure trove of information about early Christian traditions in Scotland which combines fact and legend.

2 November

Sir John Gordon was sentenced to death today, just five days after the Battle of Corrichie. Mary, Queen of Scots is believed to have watched from a window as he was beheaded in Aberdeen's Castlegate. Sir John, third son of the Earl of Huntly, was infatuated with the queen and rumoured to be her lover; some reports state she shed tears as she saw him die. The executioner was 'so awkward that he wounded Sir John several times before severing his head'.

The queen had spurned the Earl of Huntly's approaches to restore the old Catholic religion to Scotland following the recent Reformation. She further insulted the earl by ignoring his invitation to visit his castle at Huntly and was outraged when Sir John shadowed her as she travelled through Gordon lands between Aberdeen and Inverness. When the earl refused to meet the queen's demand to surrender the keys to all his castles, she declared he and Sir John outlaws. The earl, his sons and supporters marched towards Aberdeen but were defeated by the royal army at Corrichie, west of the burgh. At the moment of surrender, the elderly earl fell dead from his horse. Many of his supporters were condemned to death, including Sir John and his brother Sir George. As heir to the title, Sir George was granted a stay of execution. Sir John was less fortunate.

25 April

On this day the Privy Council of Scotland wrote to the burgh of Aberdeen regarding acts of piracy. The burgh had a long association with pirates and benefited greatly from the business they brought to the town, its harbour and its skilled shipwrights. Even prominent citizens were involved, including Provost Davidson, who had died a hero's death at Harlaw in 1411, and the Earl of Mar. Both were implicated in the capture of two English ships, one of which was owned by London Lord Mayor Richard 'Dick' Whittington. Provost Davidson had brazenly sold the stolen cargo in Amsterdam but when taken to court in Paris, he produced a Guarantee of Safe Conduct from the French Government, effectively stopping the case against him in its tracks.

In 1573 the Privy Council took action. They had decreed all men-of-war should disarm after hostilities with England had ceased. However, a certain Captain Halkerstoun had stolen a ship from Burntisland, raided the Hebrides and taken his booty to Aberdeen to sell. The Privy Council wrote to order Aberdeen's Provost and magistrates to arrest Halkerstoun's latest conquest, a Dutch ship he had captured at sea near Peterhead and sailed to Aberdeen to be prepared and rigged for further acts of piracy. Indeed, if the Aberdeen authorities refused to arrest the ship, the Privy Council would charge them with piracy along with Halkerstoun and his crew.

2 April

George Keith, fourth Earl Marischal (pronounced 'marshal') of Scotland, was a well-travelled, cultured scholar and diplomat. His hereditary title originated in 1314 at the Battle of Bannockburn, when an ancestor had been responsible for marshalling the king's cavalry.

Although King's College, originally Catholic, had become a Protestant university over twenty years earlier, in 1593 the Earl Marischal, supported by the town council and ministers of the reformed Church, established a new Protestant university within the burgh of Aberdeen.

The foundation charter for Marischal College, dated 2 April 1593, lists a wide range of subjects to be taught, including Aristotle's Ethics and Logic, Latin, Greek, geography, history, anatomy, physiology and astronomy. This 'New College', as it was called initially, was based in the old Greyfriars monastery, gifted to the Earl Marischal for the purpose by the town council. The council gave further support following a fire in the early 1600s. In 1860 Marischal and King's College united to become the University of Aberdeen. During the life of Marischal College, new granite buildings were created, most recently the famous façade, opened in 1906. Together they comprise the world's second largest granite building. Most of these college buildings, restored and modernised internally, are now used by Aberdeen City Council as its headquarters.

16 July

In this year, King James VI 'borrowed instruments of war' from Aberdeen magistrates to demolish the castles of the 'Popish Lords' who had rebelled against him. One of these was George Gordon, Earl of Huntly. The powerful Catholic Gordons had long been a problem for the Crown and the earl's seat, Huntly Castle, was blown up by Aberdeen masons in the presence of the king.

When the *Esperance* sailed into Aberdeen Harbour from Calais on this day with James Gordon and three strangers on board, the Aberdeen magistrates inevitably suspected they were Papists. They decided to seize the *Esperance* and send her passengers, guarded by twelve trustworthy Aberdonians, to Edinburgh to be handed over to the king. However, bad weather prevented their departure and the strangers were imprisoned. On 18 July, before any further action could be taken, a letter was delivered from the Gordon Laird of Auchendoun and other 'Popish Earls'. They declared their intent to attack the town instantly with fire and sword and hold the citizens to be their enemies 'in all time coming' unless the three strangers were set free. The magistrates delivered the strangers to the earls to avoid putting the citizens in 'hazert or perrell'. In October of the same year, King James VI pardoned the provost, baillies, council and inhabitants of Aberdeen for not apprehending either James Gordon or the unnamed strangers.

31 October

By the 1590s, Scotland, including Aberdeen, was in the grip of witch-hunt fever. Witchcraft had been outlawed in 1563, resulting in accusations against women whose 'poverty, sour temper or singular habits made them an object of dislike or fear'. Charged with witchcraft, sorcery and 'other diabolical or detestable practices', often by friends, neighbours or family, these women were detained and tried by the Justice Court in Aberdeen Tolbooth. A *dittay*, or list of charges, would be prepared. Those found guilty were sentenced to be *virret* – strangled. Rarely killed by the strangling, they were then burned.

Janet Wishart was denounced for taking part in a Witches Sabbath on this night, Hallowe'en, at Aberdeen's Mercat and Fish Crosses. Janet was joined by her son Thomas Lees and Isobel Cockie. Isobel was charged with playing music, on a pipe taken from the mouth of the Devil, for witches who danced in the form of hares, cats or 'other likenesses'. Janet was also accused of stealing body parts for her spells from a putrefying corpse on the gallows. In addition she was charged with casting spells which caused hens to die, her neighbour's cow to produce poison instead of milk and several people to fall ill, many suffering from a wasting disease which made them 'melt away like ane burning candle'.

Found guilty, both Janet and her son were sentenced to be burned alive.

8 August

The harbour was already well established by this day, when King James VI granted a Royal Charter to the provost and baillies of Aberdeen. By this time a cargo-handling crane had been in use for fourteen years but Aberdeen shipmasters were concerned about safety. The charter allowed income to be retained from dues charged, both on ships using the port and their goods, for a period of five years. This was to fund improvements and in 1607 a bulwark was built on the south side to help deepen the entrance. Cargoes imported and exported through the port at this time averaged 4,000 tons per year and included apples, bark, leather, iron, lime, salmon, slates and tobacco.

In 1678 Charles II granted a similar charter which allowed further improvements to be made during the 1700s and early 1800s. The North Pier, built in three stages starting in 1775, brought increased safety. Once complete, in 1879, it was more than a third of a mile long and provided shelter from easterly winds, prevented sand and shingle drifting south from the beach and enhanced the natural scour of the river. By now more than half a million tons of goods were passing through the harbour each year. Exports included products of the burgh's main industries: paper, stone, herring and soap, while goods such as tea, sugar, coal and cotton were imported.

7 February

On this day a violent snowstorm swept across Scotland. In Old Aberdeen the full force of the gale struck the crown tower of King's College Chapel and sent it crashing down through the roof of the chapel. The crown had been modelled on the crown of the Holy Roman Empire as a 'closed' imperial crown. This was believed to have been intended as a compliment, or perhaps flattery, to King James IV, the university's patron and benefactor. It was therefore extremely symbolic.

The staff were dismayed and agreed that this 'royal monument' must be restored with no delay. They all contributed what they could but could not fund repairs themselves. They therefore started an appeal for funds, which was successful in raising a sufficient amount, from lairds, the nobility and citizens of 'New Aberdeen', to contract George Thomson, 'an excellent mason of singular device'. However, the money ran out, Thomson stopped work and only a generous grant from the council of New Aberdeen allowed the rebuilding to be completed.

The crown tower has been a symbol of the university and Old Aberdeen ever since, much loved by generations of students, academics and Aberdonians.

24 June

A Royal Charter, issued on this day by Charles I, confirmed the gift of an old monastery building to Aberdeen's craftsmen, to be 'a hospital for the poor old tradesmen' of the burgh. The monastery, founded in 1181 by William the Lion, had been destroyed by fire during the Reformation. The tradesmen gave their building the name Trinity Hall after its pre-Reformation occupants, the Trinity Friars. It also became the first meeting hall of The Seven Incorporated Trades of Aberdeen.

This organisation has its origins in the trades that were most important for daily life: those which provided shelter, food and clothing. Each trade guild oversaw quality standards and supported ill or disabled members and their dependents. Today, The Seven Incorporated Trades comprise: Bakers; 'Fleshers' (butchers and slaughtermen); Weavers; Shoemakers ('Cordiners'); Tailors; Hammermen and Wrights and Coopers. Hammermen were metalworkers: cutlers, goldsmiths, blacksmiths, gunsmiths, and glaziers – glass was originally set in lead. Wrights and Coopers worked with wood and included wheelwrights, millwrights, ship-wrights, cartwrights and joiners, originally called housewrights.

In 1845, Trinity Hall and its gardens were required for the development of the railways and the organisation moved to a new Trinity Hall in Union Street. Designed by William Smith, it featured spectacular symbolic stained-glass windows. In the 1960s when The Seven Incorporated Trades moved again, their modern new Trinity Hall was designed especially to incorporate these windows.

19 June

Royalist Aberdeen fell to the Covenanters, commanded by the Marquis of Montrose, on this day.

The Royalists, led by Viscount Aboyne, had marched south and met the Covenanter Army near Stonehaven. Armed with massive cannons and other artillery, the Covenanters drove Aboyne and his men back to Aberdeen. Here the River Dee, swollen by heavy rain, was impossible to ford and the Bridge of Dee became the focus of the battle. On 18 June the Covenanters attacked with their huge cannons, dislodging large blocks of masonry from both gatehouse and bridge but killing only one Royalist. Taking the only bridge over the river was crucial to capturing the burgh and so, under cover of darkness, Montrose moved his artillery closer.

Next day, many Royalists left their posts to attend the funeral of their comrade killed the previous day. Montrose seized this opportunity and sent a few of his cavalry upriver, pretending to look for a ford. This succeeded in drawing the Royalist cavalry away from the bridge, leaving it almost undefended and vulnerable to the Covenanters' cannons. After bombarding the bridge, Montrose turned his artillery on the enemy cavalry, allowing his men to storm the bridge and take the burgh. For most of the next five years, Aberdeen was garrisoned by Covenanter troops who were the source of many complaints by citizens regarding their debauchery, drinking, fighting and swearing.

10 May

This was the day on which Aberdeen Council granted a licence to ball maker John Dickson to make and sell 'gouff ballis'. No one else was carrying out this trade in Aberdeen at the time and Dickson had testimonials from the Burgh of Leith, where golf had been played on the links since 1619.

Various early forms of golf were also played in Aberdeen before Dickson received his licence. As early as 1565, it seems from some records that golf was considered an 'unlawful amusement' in Aberdeen. In 1613, bookbinder John Allan was charged with 'setting ane goiff ball in the kirk yeard and striking the same against the kirk'. He was fined £3 for his participation in this early form of target golf. A teacher at Aberdeen Grammar School, possibly aiming to stimulate his pupils' interest in Latin, published a Latin grammar book which included golfing terms.

It is also believed that Mary, Queen of Scots played golf on Aberdeen Links. The first mention of any golf hole in Scotland, in 1625, refers to the Queen's hole on the links. By 1661 golf was played regularly on the Queen's Links and Broad Hill, today the last survivor of the sand dune system that once bordered Aberdeen beach. It seems likely that the golfers would have bought their balls from John Dickson.

13 September

Montrose had by now changed his allegiance and was leading the Royalist fight against the Covenanters. On this Friday the thirteenth he and his troops were close to Aberdeen. He sent a letter into the burgh requesting its surrender and support for the king. However, the Provost and baillies were under the close scrutiny of the Covenanter commanders and were unable to comply. As Montrose's herald and drummer boy, who had delivered the letter under the flag of truce, left the burgh, a shot rang out and the drummer boy fell dead, killed by an unidentified Covenanter musketeer.

The battle which followed centred on the approach to the Bow Brig on Aberdeen's western boundary. Here, in oatfields beside the mealmills, the Battle of Justice Mills raged on a damp and windy autumn day. It was difficult for the musketeers to keep their powder dry and smoke from gunfire blinded both sides. The smaller but more experienced Royalist force included battle-hardened Highland and Irish troops who showed no mercy in pressing home their attack. So many injured washed their wounds at the nearby Hardgate Well that it ran red with blood. The victorious Royalists then brutally sacked Aberdeen, raping women and killing every man they found. As a large Covenanter force was reported to be approaching, Montrose and his men departed. Only two days later Aberdeen was again under Covenanter control.

3 December

Aberdeen Council decreed on this day that anyone sheltering a person suspected of being ill with plague would be liable to the death penalty. With the burgh in the grip of a bubonic plague epidemic, a standing gibbet was erected in the Castlegate to emphasise the point, although the death sentence was never carried out.

Since early this year, there had been outbreaks of the disease very close to Aberdeen. Despite the plague being nearby, the guard on the burgh gates had become lax, with masters delegating the task to their servants. In May, a woman from plague-ridden Brechin travelled to Pitmuckstone, just outwith Aberdeen's western boundary. A child from Pitmuckstone was then allowed to pass the burgh gates to attend school, bringing the disease into the burgh for the first time since the early 1500s. New guards were appointed, poison was laid for vermin and middens cleared from communal areas. Strict quarantine regulations were imposed and enforced. Beyond the town gates, camps were built for victims of 'the Pestilence'. Here they were banished, to die or recover. The dead were buried in mass graves. Survivors suffered weeks of isolation in quarantine. By the end of the year 1,600 citizens were dead, a fifth of the population of Aberdeen. Although this was devastating, other towns suffered greater losses – in some places almost two-thirds of the population died.

24 May

Following eight months of siege and ten days of bombardment, on this day Governor George Ogilvy of Dunnottar Castle surrendered to the commander of Cromwell's troops. They had besieged the castle because the Honours of Scotland were being held in safekeeping there following Charles II's coronation on New Year's Day 1651.

The Honours of Scotland, which comprise the Sword of State, Sceptre and Crown, are the oldest Crown Jewels in the UK and among the oldest in the Christian world. Cromwell had already sold the precious stones from the English Crown Jewels and ordered that the metal be melted down for coin manufacture. He was enraged by Scotland's recognition of Charles II, and determined to destroy the Honours, but his troops could not force the castle's surrender until cannons arrived from the south. Unknown to Cromwell, however, the Honours had been smuggled out of the castle at least two months previously. The commander had allowed a local minister's wife, Mrs Grainger, accompanied by her maid, to visit her friend Mrs Ogilvy in the castle. When they left, the sceptre and sword, broken in two, were hidden in a bag of flax carried by the maid while the crown was concealed beneath Mrs Grainger's gown. The Honours were taken safely to Kinneff Church, where the Reverend Grainger buried them under the floor. Cromwell's troops left Dunnottar Castle empty-handed.

20 September

With swords drawn, the Earl of Mar and fellow Jacobite lords rode into Aberdeen on this day and at the Mercat Cross proclaimed James Francis Edward Stuart to be King James VIII and III of England.

The Jacobite cause had its roots in the revolution of 1689, after Catholic James VII of Scotland and II of England fled to France. His Protestant daughter Mary and her husband William reigned over both Scotland and England. Mary's younger sister, Anne, also a Protestant, succeeded them. When Queen Anne died in 1714 with no surviving children, the only direct heir to the throne was her Catholic half-brother James, who had been born and brought up in France. His supporters were named Jacobites from *Jacobus*, the Latin form of his name. As a Catholic king was unacceptable to both Scottish and English parliaments, the closest Protestant heir, James VI and I of England's great-grandson, the Elector of Hanover, became King George I.

There was considerable support for James in Aberdeen and Aberdeenshire and the Jacobite Standard was raised by the Earl of Mar in Braemar in early September 1715. Unfortunately, the Jacobites lacked a commander for their 12,000-strong army. Neither the Earl of Mar nor 'King' James were military leaders; the Rising of 1715 foundered. Many Jacobite supporters lost everything – their castles were burned, property was forfeited and families fled into exile. The Jacobite cause, however, lived on.

6 March

In 1743 James VIII of Scotland and III of England proclaimed his son Charles Edward Stuart, 'Bonnie Prince Charlie', to be regent. The young prince's arrival in Scotland in 1745 strengthened support for the Jacobite cause. When the government's redcoat soldiers left Aberdeen they had taken all arms and ammunition with them. A rebel council was elected and started to raise money and arms for the Jacobites. Many citizens loyal to the government sent messages requesting help but the redcoats sent were defeated by Jacobites at Inverurie.

In February 1746 government troops arrived in force in Aberdeen under the command of the Duke of Cumberland, youngest son of King George II. The Jacobite council was forced out of office and a new pro-government council elected. On this day Cumberland was appointed a Burgess of Aberdeen and the names of all Jacobite burgesses were struck from the register. He lodged in a 200-year-old mansion, now known as Provost Skene's House. Twenty-one regiments of redcoats commandeered the recently built, but as yet unoccupied, Robert Gordon's Hospital, its gardens and the surrounding land. Their horses were stabled nearby in the disused West Church of St Nicholas. In April the government troops left Aberdeen in pursuit of the Jacobites and on Culloden Moor, near Inverness, the redcoats finally defeated the heavily outnumbered Jacobites. A large number of surviving rebels were slaughtered on the orders of 'Butcher' Cumberland.

29 December

Aberdeen's Journal was first published on this day. It cost tuppence; town subscribers were assured of delivery by noon on the day of publishing. In 1748 the paper changed its name to the *Aberdeen Journal* and was owned and edited by the Chalmers family until the mid-1800s. In 1830 it was the first Scottish paper to use steam for its presses. Two years later it had a circulation of 2,231 copies per week, many more than either *The Scotsman* or the *Glasgow Herald*. A staunchly Conservative paper, its circulation stalled following the launch of the Liberal *Aberdeen Free Press* in 1853. The *Aberdeen Journal* remained a weekly publication until 1876. One reason given for this was that: 'the proverbial frugality, amounting almost to parsimony, of the inhabitants of this part of the kingdom, prevents any paper published more frequently than once a week, from obtaining a circulation of any considerable extent.'

In 1922, following its amalgamation with its rival, the *Aberdeen Free Press*, the *Aberdeen Journal* became *The Press and Journal*. This, affectionately known locally as *The P&J*, is the main newspaper for the north of Scotland, published in six geographic editions six days per week. *The P&J* is the source of many urban myths, most unjustified. One story, much-loved by Aberdonians but incorrect, is that, following the sinking of the *Titanic*, the newspaper's front page headline was 'North East Man Drowns at Sea.'

25 December

This was the day an order came into force banning men and boys in Scotland from wearing 'those parts of highland dress commonly called the plaid, philabeg, or little kilt'. Only soldiers serving the king were permitted to wear tartan. The penalty was either six months' imprisonment without bail or 'being compelled to become a soldier'.

The order was enforced, particularly in areas which had supported the Jacobite risings in 1715 and 1745. The following April seven or eight men were brought into Aberdeen under military escort from Cromar, around 30 miles to the west. Their crime was 'wearing highland garb'. Two years later, a man known as William Gow or Smith, who was said to have supported the '45, arrived at a house in the Cabrach, in the hills south-west of Huntly, to find two soldiers stationed there. The corporal challenged him for wearing tartan and in the scuffle which followed, Gow struck the corporal several times. When the soldiers drew their muskets, Gow fled into the house and slammed the door. Shooting through the door, the soldiers killed him. Private Thomas Stables was later found guilty by a jury which recommended mercy but which sentenced him to be hanged. A short time before his planned execution, he received a free pardon from the king, as he had been 'provoked into (the murder) in the discharge of his duty'.

10 July

In 1680, 12-year-old Robert Gordon inherited £1,000 from his father, an Edinburgh advocate. Three years later he was elected a Burgess of Guild, which entitled him to trade as a merchant in goods he had not manufactured. After graduating from Marischal College, he travelled in Europe and set up in business as a merchant trader in Danzig, now Gdańsk. An early indication of his success was the generous contribution he made towards the rebuilding of Marischal College in 1692. Around 1720 he returned to Aberdeen, where he continued to trade and also to lend money. As he had no wife or children he bequeathed his considerable fortune to found a 'hospital', or residential school, to educate the sons and grandsons of Burgesses of Aberdeen. When he died in 1731, his body lay in state at Marischal College. He was then honoured with a public funeral and burial in the kirk of St Nicholas.

Prior to his death he had chosen the site where the Blackfriars Friary had once stood as the location for the school. He had also given precise instructions about how the school should be organised and operated. The building, designed by William Adam, was completed but not yet in use when it was commandeered by government troops in 1746. Finally, with military damage repaired, Robert Gordon's Hospital opened to its first thirteen pupils on this day.

24 July

This was the day when the Lords refused an appeal by Gideon Duncan, weaver, of Old Aberdeen. His crime was causing a disturbance in church by singing out of tune. The magistrate who had tried him, Professor Gordon of King's College, had a vested interest in the case.

Until this time, the singing of psalms was described as lugubrious with drawling tunes. New thinking, supported by the professors and principals of King's College, introduced singing in parts – bass, tenor and treble. One of General Wolfe's soldiers, who had successfully taught this part-singing in Monymusk, was released from his army duties to instruct the singers of King's College Chapel. Gideon was one of these, had a good strong voice and was a great supporter of reformed church music. However, the rest of the congregation sang as they always had, resulting in such a cacophony that Gideon changed sides. One Sunday, he organised a rebellion with others who had been taught the new music. Standing in the body of the kirk, directly in front of the precentor, he sang in the old way and, with his friends, created a 'tumult in the Church'. His sentence, upheld by the Lords, was a fine of £50 Scots plus £6 Scots expenses. He was also ordered to keep the peace. Furthermore, he was imprisoned until he paid his fine.

3 December

Peter Williamson was one of 600 children sent abroad illegally from Aberdeen as indentured servants in the 1740s. People who sold their indentures at this time were given a cash payment in return for agreeing to work as servants for a specified period in America. There they were sold to the highest bidder, very often a plantation owner.

Merchants specialising in this legal slave trade also bought children from kidnappers. Parents often found it impossible to reclaim their abducted children as the Town Clerk and magistrates were directly involved in this illegal trade. When 12-year-old Peter was abducted in Aberdeen in 1743, his brother and father searched for him without success. After surviving appalling shipboard conditions and a shipwreck, Peter was sold in Philadelphia to a Scottish plantation owner. He treated Peter kindly and educated him in return for additional years' indenture. When he died, Peter gained his freedom early and inherited money. Following several adventurous years in America, Peter returned to Britain and published a book about his life. The Aberdeen magistrates, outraged by his accusations about them, falsely tried and imprisoned him. After his release, he brought legal proceedings in Edinburgh against the Aberdeen Town Clerk and magistrates responsible for his kidnapping and enforced indenture. On this day, twenty-five years after his abduction, Peter finally got justice and was awarded £200 damages and 100 guineas costs.

26 December

By this time, wool combing was one of Aberdeen's main industries. Skilled wool combers were well paid and enjoyed special privileges, including processions and celebrations on the day of their patron saint. Many apparently only worked four days per week, requiring the other three 'to imbibe alcohol'. Around 1768 their league, or union, refused to continue training apprentices in order to protect their own interests. However, Alexander Frost broke away from the union and resumed apprenticeship teaching. His shop was broken into twice at night. His wool and tools were destroyed and on the second occasion his fire-pot was overturned and the flames fed with wool and oil. Magistrates and wool manufacturers offered rewards totalling £40 with no result.

On this night, members of the wool-combers union swore on the Bible to murder Frost. Some went to his house at dead of night but, clad only in his nightshirt, he escaped through a window. They then recruited ex-soldier John Gibbons and others to watch him and stab him to death. Fortunately the conspiracy was uncovered and Gibbons and six wool-combers were apprehended a month after their sworn oath to kill Frost. The following May the court found five guilty of conspiracy and sentenced them to ten years' transportation to the plantations. The other two, including Gibbons, were found guilty of conspiracy and assault and banished for life to the plantations.

14 November

Samuel Seabury of Connecticut was consecrated the first bishop of the American Episcopal Church on this day in Aberdeen. As there were no bishops in America, Seabury, rector of St Peter's church, Westchester, New York, had to travel to England for his consecration. However, as an American citizen, he could not take the oath of allegiance to the king. At this time the Episcopal Church in Scotland was repressed and did not recognise the Hanovarian monarchy, so Bishop Seabury could be consecrated in Scotland. The ceremony took place in Bishop Skinner's private chapel in Longacre, Aberdeen, where Marischal College and Greyfriars church now stand.

From 1817, Aberdeen had a lovely Episcopal cathedral, designed by local architect Archibald Simpson. In the 1920s there were plans for a grand new cathedral to commemorate the 150th anniversary of Seabury's consecration. The bishop and cathedral's provost travelled across the Atlantic to raise funds for this in the USA. However, this proved impossible due to events which happened while they were at sea: they arrived to news of the Wall Street Crash. Later, a different commemoration was planned, to extend and beautify the existing St Andrew's Cathedral. The American Communion generously supported heraldic decorations on the ceilings of the north and south aisles, featuring the crests of the American states. Although delayed by the Second World War, the Seabury Memorial was finally dedicated in 1948.

1787

1 June

The Castlegate, Aberdeen's market place, saw its last execution on this day. The last person to be hanged there was William Webster, a vagrant ex-soldier who had been banished for swindling people with his Wheel of Fortune. Later, he was arrested in the countryside for theft and housebreaking. He admitted to the theft, but pled not guilty to housebreaking.

The case centred on the evidence of a young girl whose linen gown had been stolen during the housebreaking. A gown which had been found in Webster's possession was produced in court as evidence. Initially, the girl could not swear it was hers as it was similar in style and fabric to those worn by many others. Webster asked if she would try it on, possibly thinking that the gown might be too small if the girl had grown during the months he waited for trial. As she started to put it on, she found a tiny bloodstain on a seam, made when she had pricked her finger while sewing it. This allowed her to positively identify the gown as her property. Webster was found guilty and sentenced to hang. While in prison, his wife brought him a saw, but his attempted escape was thwarted. He later tried to take his own life, but the spirits, laudanum, opium and razor he had obtained were confiscated. He was hanged according to his sentence.

14 December

Aberdeen Medical Society was founded today by medical students led by James Robertson and James McGrigor, who later became Director General of the Army Medical Department. At this time the students were dissatisfied with the quality of their teaching, partly because their anatomy studies required them to spend a year in Edinburgh. The society's meetings initially focused on anatomy and dissection. Later, medical students turned to grave robbing for bodies to dissect. Society minutes record fines for those shirking body-snatching duty and payments of half a guinea made to those who delivered a corpse.

As the society became established its reputation grew, medical practitioners joined and strengthened its membership. The name changed to 'Aberdeen Medico-Chirugical Society' and by 1820 its magnificent Medical Hall, at the south end of King Street, was complete. Designed by renowned Aberdeen architect Archibald Simpson, it cost £3,000.

The Society has played an important, often unseen, role in the health of Aberdeen's citizens, advising the council during epidemics and planning, in the 1920s, a hospital and medical school complex at Foresterhill. This is now one of the largest integrated health campuses in Europe. It is home to the 'Med-Chi', its modern Medical Hall, valuable collection of books, medical instruments and artefacts dating back to the 1700s. Education is still fundamental to the Society, which offers clinical and scientific lectures for members and bursaries to medical undergraduates.

24 June

This was the day on which the 100th Regiment of Foot, later the Gordon Highlanders, first paraded in Aberdeen. At this time of social unrest and uncertainty, the British Government and the king perceived post-revolutionary France to be a significant threat.

The army desperately needed more men and King George III requested that regiments be raised throughout the United Kingdom. In north-east Scotland the Duke of Gordon responded. He considered his son, the Marquess of Huntly who was a lieutenant colonel in the army, to be the ideal commander for the new regiment. Enlistment was initially slow, despite the reward of 'the king's shilling' and pay of a shilling a day – six times the wage of a skilled tradesman. However, the Duchess of Gordon, determined that her son's regiment would be successful, decided to take action herself and toured local markets and fairs with her daughters. Known as Duchess Jean, she was forthright, outspoken and stunningly beautiful. She rewarded recruits with the king's shilling and also with a kiss. Legend has it that she sometimes also had a golden guinea between her lips. Recruitment improved dramatically.

As the recruits paraded on this day, they believed they were leaving Aberdeen and the north-east to fight the French and Napoleon. However, the following day they sailed from Aberdeen Harbour to Southampton and very unexciting, but relatively safe, garrison duty in the Mediterranean.

21 April

Surgeon Alexander Gordon had been appointed to Aberdeen Dispensary in 1786. He was a specialist in obstetrics, had trained in Leiden and London and had experience as a surgeon's mate in the Royal Navy. Today, in the *Aberdeen Journal*, his *Treatise on Child-bed Fever* was advertised for sale.

From December 1789 to March 1792, epidemics of erysipelas and puerperal (child-bed) fever occurred simultaneously in Aberdeen. Alexander's meticulous record keeping allowed him to deduce that the diseases were not only related but were spread by medical attendants. This was groundbreaking work at a time when physicians blamed epidemics on bad air or 'miasma'. Once Alexander started washing between attending patients, fumigating his clothes and burning contaminated items, the number of his patients who died from puerperal fever dropped dramatically to 33 per cent. At this time, the accepted mortality rate was 68-100 per cent. However, in his *Treatise* he followed the common practice of the time, giving the names of both patients and medical attendants to ensure credibility. His medical colleagues were extremely hostile and effectively ostracised him. His discovery of the transmission of infection by poor hygiene predated by fifty years the 'discoveries' of later physicians who advocated similar preventative measures.

Early in 1796 he left his family and Aberdeen to return to the Royal Navy. He died in 1799 aged only 47. His twin brother, an Aberdeenshire farmer, lived for another forty-two years.

1 April

This day dawned clear and calm but by nightfall forty-two men were dead in one of the worst shipwrecks Aberdeen had ever seen. Only two survived.

The *Oscar* was one of five whalers preparing to depart for the Greenland whaling grounds. As they lay at anchor in Aberdeen Bay a violent snowstorm blew up, with the wind quickly escalating to hurricane force. One ship weighed anchor to ride out the storm while three returned to harbour. Unfortunately the *Oscar*'s master waited too long before weighing anchor, leaving the ship no room to manoeuvre and she was driven onto the rocks to the south of the harbour at Greyhope Bay. The crew cut down the main mast to bridge the gap between the ship and the rocky shore, but it fell sideways and was useless. The fore and mizzen masts were blown down, taking with them the men clinging to the rigging.

The crowd, which had gathered to watch the whalers depart, was horror-struck and powerless to help as sailors were washed overboard. One was lucky to be carried towards the shore where he was pulled to safety. Although the presence of a lighthouse could not have prevented the loss of the *Oscar* and her crew, this disaster resulted in renewed calls for a lighthouse to be built to the south of the harbour. Twenty years later, Girdleness Lighthouse was built.

1 June

Aberdeen Golf Club was formed on this day. Its members played on the Queen's Links and over the Broad Hill, the last remaining sand dune of the system which originally lined Aberdeen Bay.

The club's predecessor was the Society of Golfers at Aberdeen, formed in 1780, making this the world's sixth oldest golf club. In common with other early golf clubs, its members were Freemasons who preferred not to keep written records, therefore few details are known from that time. However, it is known that in 1783 the Society was the first to introduce the Five Minute Rule which restricted the time allowed to search for golf balls.

The Queen's Links was shared with cricketers and football players and in 1886 the club captain proposed developing a private course at Balgownie. Originally designed by Archie and Robert Simpson of Carnoustie, the course was later lengthened and re-bunkered by James Braid. In 1903 the club became Royal Aberdeen Golf Club, the title granted by King Edward VII to recognise Prince Leopold's patronage in 1872.

The present-day Balgownie Course challenges good golfers with variable conditions and a classic links layout, out through the dunes and back along a plateau. It was a popular, if testing, venue for the British Seniors Open in 2005, the Walker Cup in 2011 and its first major European Tour event, the Scottish Open, in 2014.

5 June

This was the day on which a large mob, 'not falling short of half a thousand', attacked the White Ship, a house of ill repute run by Meggie Dickie. As it stood where St Nicholas Street meets Union Street today, it was convenient for sailors coming into town from the harbour and also 'allured the unthinking, as they passed the spot'.

The town was busy with Aberdonians celebrating the birthday of King George III when four young men attacked the brothel, which they found offensive. They broke down the door, 'maltreated the faces of the backsliding young women' inside and mistreated Meggie herself. A large mob joined them to gut the house and burn the furniture in the street. One man smashed Meggie's 'excellent eight-day clock' with an axe. A military unit was called out to break up the riot and apprehend the ringleaders. John Douglas, the most actively involved, was sentenced to be transported for seven years and two others were sentenced to twelve months in Aberdeen's Bridewell Prison. The case against the fourth offender was not proven. It is not clear whether Meggie Dickie was also punished. Certainly at this time, 'a loose woman' who kept 'a bawdy house' could expect banishment and, if she had not moved away within the period specified by the court, she would have been whipped in public by the 'common hangman'.

21 February

In 1794 Charles Abercrombie, commissioned by Aberdeen's magistrates, reported on access to the city from north and south. He advocated new, wide direct streets: one from the south-west to connect with the market place in Castle Street and another leading south to enter the north side of Castle Street.

The Act of Parliament, required to proceed with this, was passed in 1800. Trustees were appointed to acquire the land and obtain designs. Land purchase proved complicated, particularly for the street from the south-west. The trustees unanimously agreed this should be called Union Street while that leading from the north would be King Street.

King Street progressed well but the topography of the land proved problematic for Union Street. Plans to bridge the Denburn Valley had to be redrawn by the project's superintendent, Thomas Fletcher, and advice sought from Thomas Telford. On the suggestion of the contractor, it was agreed the bridge should be lengthened at additional cost; it would become the longest stone arch in Britain. These delays resulted in longer loans and higher interest payments. Aberdonians showed little initial interest in taking up feus on the new streets, resulting in less income than planned. On this day, the inevitable happened when a meeting of creditors of the Treasurer of the City effectively declared the council bankrupt. In 1819 the council was again bankrupt as a result of the development.

26 June

John Fyfe was born on this day, the son of a quarry owner. By his early twenties, John had leased part of the quarrying on Paradise Hill, Kemnay. However, primitive equipment prevented the exploitation of the best stone, which could be obtained only by quarrying downwards rather than on the cliff face. Legend has it that, while sitting in church and mentally using the pulpit and gallery as anchor points, John invented the aerial ropeway; this became known as the 'Scotch Steam Derrick' or 'the Blondin'. It was based on a rope-and-pulley contraption he had seen a Deeside postman use to carry mail across the river. John's invention, first used at Kemnay, revolutionised the quarrying industry.

John Fyfe went to great lengths to find markets for his granite and keep his men in work. Kemnay granite, exported from Aberdeen Harbour, was used to build several London bridges and the Embankment. This kept 500 of John's masons in work for seven years. Believing insufficient granite was available, the architects of Aberdeen's new Town House specified sandstone but John intervened and guaranteed supplies. As a result, the Town House was built of silver Kemnay granite. When he died, the *Aberdeen Free Press* wrote: 'Aberdeen itself owes Mr Fyfe a lasting debt of gratitude ... for his public-spirited generosity in making it possible ... to retain inviolate the most striking aspect of Aberdeen as the Granite City.'

19 December

On this day two boys playing near Andrew Moir's anatomy theatre watched a dog dig up the remains of a human limb. Aberdeen had no professional grave robbers or 'resurrectionists' as there was limited demand for bodies at this time. The requirement for bodies for dissection in Aberdeen therefore had to be met by medical students themselves, motivated not by greed but by 'a sincere and honest study of anatomy'.

By 1831 many graveyards had watch-houses from where bereaved families could guard the new graves of their loved ones. In many churchyards heavy mort-stones were placed on top of the grave, or iron mort-safes were buried over the coffin, to prevent robbers stealing the body. Each of these deterrents was left in place for six weeks, by which time the body was too putrefied for anatomists' use. Despite these precautions, fresh bodies were still taken regularly and Aberdonians were appalled by the practice.

As news of the dog's gruesome find spread around the town, an angry crowd of around 2,000 gathered at the anatomy theatre. Anger turned to fury and the mob broke into the theatre, ejected Moir and his students and chased them through the streets. Three bodies laid out for dissection were recovered before windows were smashed and the theatre set on fire. Soldiers brought to restore order stood and watched as the building was razed to the ground.

15 October

At sunset on this evening, Girdleness Lighthouse shone for the first time. Following the wreck of the whaler *Oscar* twenty years previously, the shipmasters of Aberdeen had campaigned for a lighthouse to be built on Girdle Ness to the south of the Dee estuary and the harbour.

The lighthouse, designed by Robert Stevenson, had enclosed grazing for cows and a walled garden to provide keepers with fresh milk and vegetables. The 37m-high tower was built to a new design with two distinct fixed lights, a single one at the top and a lower light which comprised thirteen lamps inside a glazed gallery. This allowed sailors to differentiate Girdleness from the two existing lighthouses on the north-east coast. The top light, 59m above sea level, was later enlarged and in 1870 Girdleness was used successfully to test the use of pressurised paraffin vapour to fuel the light. The use of paraffin became normal practice and lighthouse-keepers became known as 'paraffin oilers'. By 1890, with a clockwork turntable installed enabling the upper light to flash, the lower light was discontinued. The lighthouse was automated in 1991.

Girdleness Lighthouse's 'character' is two flashes of 200,000-candlepower white light every twenty seconds which can be seen 22 miles (50km) out to sea. It is now one of three Scottish lighthouses providing transmissions for the public DGPS satellite-based navigation system.

6 June

Thomas Blake Glover, son of a coastguard, was born on this day in Fraserburgh. The family later moved to the coastguard station at Bridge of Don, Aberdeen, from where Thomas walked to school in Old Aberdeen.

At the age of 21, Thomas set off for the Far East. In Nagasaki, the only international port in Japan at this time, he built a good business exporting tea, but soon took advantage of opportunities offered by the rebellion against the Shogun. He prospered by selling ships and arms to the rebels, thus helping to restore Japan's rightful ruler. He introduced mechanised coal mining, was a founding partner in the Kirin Brewery and imported ships from Aberdeen; these became the basis of the Japanese navy. A dry dock was also ordered from Aberdeen and installed at Nagasaki shipyard. For forty years he was international business adviser to the founders of Mitsubishi. He assisted several young Japanese Samurai to travel to the West to study, some of whom attended his old school, the Gymnasium in Old Aberdeen. His contribution to the modernisation and industrialisation of Japan was recognised in 1908 when he became the first non-Japanese to be appointed to the Order of the Rising Sun by the emperor.

Known as 'the Scottish Samurai', his personal life is believed to have inspired the story for Puccini's 'Madam Butterfly'.

4 October

The newly-widened Bridge of Dee was formally opened on this day. On his death more than 300 years earlier, Bishop Elphinstone had left a £20,000 bequest to ensure the stone bridge he had planned would be built over the River Dee. Bishop Gavin Dunbar continued the work of his predecessor, using the dressed Moray sandstone already obtained by Elphinstone. The bridge was completed in 1527, providing travellers with a safe crossing over the River Dee, one of the fastest-flowing rivers in Scotland. Until then, the only option for horsemen and wagons was to ford the river.

The cutwaters between each of the bridge's seven arches easily withstood the force of the river, even when in spate. The roadway above was flat but only around 4m wide and by 1840 the City Architect, John Smith, recommended it be replaced. The town council did not agree and ordered that the bridge should be widened rather than replaced. The facings, which had been restored in the 1700s, were carefully removed on the western side. Once a new section had been added to this upstream side, the facings were rebuilt and the bridge, now twice as wide, appeared little different from previously. Even the old pedestrian refuges on the roadway were retained. The bridge remains in constant use today, albeit with a width restriction to prevent use by large vehicles.

7 September

The royal yacht *Victoria and Albert* was sighted this morning in Aberdeen Bay, causing consternation ashore. The royal party was not expected until the following day and ceremonial arrangements were incomplete. The queen stayed on board while Prince Albert came ashore to visit the universities and a granite works.

Punctually at 8.30 a.m. the following day, a salute was fired and Queen Victoria, Prince Albert and their three eldest children stepped ashore. A cheering crowd, estimated at 80,000, had come to see the first reigning monarch to visit Aberdeen for almost 200 years. The royal family passed under a triumphal arch on Waterloo Quay and were accompanied to the municipal boundary by the town council and magistrates. With 'flags and triumphal arches everywhere', the royal carriages passed through Banchory, Kincardine O'Neil and Aboyne, crossed the River Dee at Ballater and arrived at Balmoral Castle at a quarter to three.

This was their first visit to Balmoral, which the queen described as 'a pretty little castle in the old Scotch style'. She had been told about the Dee Valley's dry climate and obtained the Balmoral lease without having visited. However, the castle was not large enough for her family and royal entourage and, after Prince Albert had bought the estate, they planned a larger castle. The queen laid the foundation stone in September 1853. Three years later their magnificent new castle was complete.

12 September

Queen Victoria visited the Gathering at Braemar Castle on this day. There she watched the traditional contests of putting the stone, throwing the hammer, tossing the caber and a hill race, won comfortably by her ghillie, Duncan. Later, local children danced in the castle for the queen.

It is believed that Braemar is the historic home of all Highland Gatherings. King Malcolm III, who ruled Scotland from 1058 for thirty-five years, is said to have held the first-ever Highland Games here. The games were based on practical requirements. Some competitions were to find the strongest men and also to identify the fastest sprinters and men who could run long distances over the hills to deliver messages reliably. Later, when clan chieftains raised their own armies, new competitions were added to find the best pipers to lead the men into battle and the best dancers who would dance to celebrate victory. The most famous event of all, tossing the caber, determines which strong men can control their strength best – the winner is not the man who can throw the caber farthest, but who can toss it to fall, top over bottom, in a straight line.

Today, there are Gatherings for Highland Games throughout Scotland with many in and around Aberdeen. Each year members of the royal family attend the Braemar Royal Highland Gathering, on the first Saturday in September.

13 July

This was the first day of judging at the Royal Agricultural Society Show at Windsor Home Park, watched by Queen Victoria and Prince Albert. William McCombie, of Tillyfour near Alford (pronounced 'áfford'), Aberdeenshire, swept the board in the Scotch Polled cattle classes. All the winners were either bred by him or were animals he owned and had obtained from Hugh Watson of Keillor.

Hugh Watson and William McCombie are credited with founding the world-famous Aberdeen-Angus cattle breed, descended from the hardy, black hornless 'polled' cattle native to north-east Scotland. McCombie founded his herd predominantly from Watson's Keillor bloodlines and showed widely the outstanding cattle he produced. Sir George Macpherson-Grant of Ballindalloch spent fifty years refining the breed, also winning significant prizes with cattle from his herd, the oldest in the world. These breed pioneers documented their beasts' breeding, or pedigrees, even before the Herd Book was established in 1862.

Aberdeen-Angus beef is particularly flavoursome due to the slight marbling of fat through the meat. It is much sought after by chefs and the breed is now well established around the world. It is, however, in Alford near the breed's birthplace that a magnificent sculpture of an Aberdeen-Angus bull now commemorates the breed's early history. It was unveiled by Prince Charles in 2001. Queen Elizabeth the Queen Mother, at that time patron of the Aberdeen-Angus Cattle Society, accompanied him.

15 September

From 1593 until this day, Aberdeen had two universities, King's College and Marischal College. Aberdonians have long enjoyed boasting about this fact, as during this 267-year period there were only two universities in England.

There was considerable rivalry between King's and Marischal colleges throughout this time; brief fusion in the 1600s did not last for long. During the 1700s most Marischal students came from the burgh of 'New Aberdeen' and Aberdeenshire, while King's, strictly residential, took undergraduates from the Highlands as well as Aberdeenshire. Each college regularly poached the other's students, although during the Enlightenment, from the mid-1700s, academics from both universities were active members of 'The Wise Club', Aberdeen's philosophical society. Despite this, there were regular court cases brought by each college against the other and, with no chancellor to adjudicate, many squabbling King's academics also took each other to court.

A series of Royal Commissions in the early 1800s examined all British universities, looking at all the Scottish institutions together. With great changes in England and a new university in Wales, Scottish graduates had to be able to compete – and their degrees had to be fit for purpose. At last, on this day, the universities were united to form the University of Aberdeen. At this time, arts and divinity were taught at King's while medicine and law students attended Marischal.

22 August

Thermopylae was launched today from the Aberdeen shipyard of Walter Hood & Co. She was a tea clipper built for the Aberdeen White Star Line.

The 'Aberdeen' or 'clipper bow' was a revolutionary new design developed by Alexander Hall & Co. It allowed ships to carry more sail, improving both speed and performance. The name clipper came from 'clipping time' off the journey; speed was vital to bring tea quickly from China to the West. The first ship to arrive with the new season's tea was assured of the best prices. Britain's first tea clipper was *Stornoway*, also built in Aberdeen by Alexander Hall & Co. By the time *Thermopylae* was launched, tea races between clippers were well established and huge bets would ride on which ship would arrive first in the Thames.

Thermopylae was a record-breaker from the start. Her maiden voyage was from London to Melbourne via Shanghai and the tea port of Fouchow. This she achieved in sixty-three days or sixty days 'pilot to pilot' and broke records on all sections of her voyage. In 1872 she raced the most famous tea clipper of all, *Cutty Sark*, from Shanghai to London and won after *Cutty Sark* lost her rudder. She once crossed the Pacific in a world-record twenty-nine days, kept pace for three days with a fast steam liner and her record day's run was 380 statute miles.

5 April

On this annual holiday there was a large fair in Torry, on the south side of the River Dee, which attracted many Aberdonians from the north side of the river. Long queues built up for the ferry boat which operated across the harbour by means of a pulley and hawser. The boat was certified for thirty-two seated passengers but on this busy holiday as many as possible crowded on board. On what became the boat's last trip, there were seventy passengers, many of them standing, and children were tucked into every available space.

In early April the River Dee often becomes swollen with melting snow from the Grampian and Cairngorm mountains to the west. The river in spate, coupled with a strong flood tide, causes an exceptionally strong and dangerous current. Just such a current caught the overloaded ferry boat in mid-stream, causing panic on board. The boat started taking water and, in a vain attempt to avert disaster, the hawser was cut, but this did not prevent the boat capsizing. All the passengers and the ferryman were washed overboard into the treacherous icy water and many were swept away by the current. Thirty-two people, many of them children, perished. Aberdeen's citizens were appalled and demanded that a long-planned bridge be built over the Dee at Torry. It was opened only five years later.

2 July

Five years after the River Dee ferry disaster a fine new bridge was formally opened on this day, at last providing a safe crossing between Aberdeen and Torry. Until this day only a suspension bridge some distance upstream linked the rural area on the south bank with Ferryhill in Aberdeen.

In 1868, the River Dee was diverted into the artificial channel where it still flows through the harbour today. As part of this project, which included development to the south of the river, Aberdeen Corporation intended to build a bridge. However, these proposals foundered and no action was taken until after the ferry disaster of 1876. Following this, the Corporation was forced to defer to public opinion and funds were made available from the Bridge of Don Endowment Fund, administered by the Corporation. It seemed probable that the new bridge would be built with iron girders, as was usual at this time. However, John Fyfe of Kemnay Quarry submitted a price, thousands of pounds lower than any other, for a granite bridge, in keeping with Aberdeen's growing reputation as 'the Granite City'. The five-arched bridge, designed by Edward Blyth and named the Victoria Bridge, was constructed of Kemnay granite and was heavily subsidised by John Fyfe. Two-thirds of the £26,000 cost was met from the Endowment Fund. Aberdonians, horrified by the ferry disaster, also contributed.

27 September

On this rainy Thursday, Union Street was bedecked with flags and flowers to greet the arrival of Princess Beatrice from Balmoral. At the Music Hall, she officially opened a bazaar to raise funds for the sick children's hospital. Later a huge procession, which included five marching bands, influential Aberdonians and organisations, accompanied the princess's carriage to Duthie Park.

The Duthies were a well-known Aberdeen shipbuilding family. Miss Elizabeth Crombie Duthie had gifted land to the city to create a public park in memory of her father and brother. The park included a grass area suitable for cricket, floral beds, mature and newly planted trees and space for all to benefit from healthy fresh air. Miss Duthie presented the princess with a symbolic silver key for the park gates. Having declared the park open, Princess Beatrice then handed the key to the Lord Provost before planting a tree to mark the occasion. As she did so, the crowd surged forward. Crush barriers gave way. Everyone, including the princess, remained calm but schoolchildren at the front were too disorganised to sing 'God Save the Queen' as planned.

Duthie Park has recently been restored to its Victorian grandeur. There is a bandstand by the cricket pitch, a huge indoor garden – the David Welch Winter Gardens – and a statue of Hygeia, goddess of health and cleanliness, as a memorial to Miss Duthie.

12 June

A Royal Warrant issued on this day confirmed Chivas Brothers as Purveyors of Grocery to Her Majesty Queen Victoria at Aberdeen. James Chivas and a previous business partner had long supplied the queen. The company was also a recognised supplier to her eldest son, the Prince of Wales, her mother, the Duchess of Kent, and the Emperor of Austria. Chivas also 'purveyed' a great deal more than groceries, at different times providing a cricket ball, 'long woollen drawers' for a royal page and 'a quiet young donkey' to pull the queen's invalid carriage.

James Chivas and his son Alexander, who at this time had recently joined the business, continued to supply wines and spirits to the royal households and other prestigious visitors from their King Street shop. However, supplies of wine and brandy had become scarce due to the decimation of French vineyards by aphids in the 1860s and many Englishmen were turning to whisky. Already a pioneer of whisky blending, James realised that his discerning customers had fine palates and harsh young malt whiskies were not to their taste. He therefore sourced better, more mature whiskies to blend. His first brand, Royal Glendee, quickly became popular both locally and farther afield. Today, the Chivas name is best known for the blended Scotch whisky Chivas Regal, one of the world's favourite whiskies. This was first blended by Chivas Brothers of Aberdeen.

27 July

This was the day on which Thomas Jaffray Lawrence married his sweetheart, Jane Duguid. Both were paper mill workers from Woodside, Aberdeen, but this was no ordinary local wedding. Thomas had been living and working in the USA for six or seven years and following the wedding they both travelled back to Massachusetts.

By the late 1870s, Aberdeen was leading the world in paper production with several mills by the River Don at Woodside. The largest was producing 12 tons of paper daily, making it the most productive in the world. The city's paper mills were especially renowned for their envelope production; many years later, the first self-sealing envelope was produced in Aberdeen.

The world's second largest producer was William Whiting of Holyoke, Massachusetts. There, a recently built second mill had increased total production to 11 tons per day, including fine-quality writing and envelope paper. More skilled workers were required to sustain production and Whiting looked to the Woodside mills for recruitment. Thomas Lawrence, aged 20, was head-hunted and travelled off to a new life in Holyoke where he became supervisor of the new number two mill. When he returned to claim his bride, his marriage certificate described him as 'Paper Maker'; his new wife was merely a 'Paper Mill Worker'. Thomas and Jane were just two of many paper workers who travelled to a new life in America.

13 December

The recently incorporated Rubislaw Granite Company today bought 20 acres of ground, including Rubislaw Quarry, plant, stone stock and business goodwill, from William Gibb. Gibb, the sole remaining partner in John Gibb & Son, quarry owners and quarry masters, was forced to sell due to ill-health. A prospectus, issued by the company to raise share capital, stated: 'the celebrity of Rubislaw Granite, from its unsurpassed suitability for the highest class of polished Granite work ... secured a steadily progressive demand for this valuable stone during the past fifty years'.

Stone had been taken from the Hill of Rubislaw for much longer than fifty years. From about 1680, people helped themselves to stone for building, from this and other locations. But granite is an exceptionally hard and heavy stone, extremely difficult to cut and dress. As a result it was not until steam was used to power cutting and polishing machinery and 'the Blondin' was introduced that the industry achieved success. At this time many local quarries provided stone for almost all new buildings in Aberdeen, which became known as 'the Granite City'. The Hill of Rubislaw became the largest of all the quarries, also producing stone for Sevastopol Harbour and buildings in Edinburgh, London and Paris. When it closed in 1971, no longer economically viable due to its size, it was the largest man-made hole in Europe, 142m deep and 120m across.

14 May

Piper George Findlater from Forgue, Aberdeenshire, was decorated by Queen Victoria in person on this day. While a patient in Netley Military Hospital, Hampshire, he received the Victoria Cross for his outstanding bravery in October 1897 on the North West Frontier between India and Afghanistan. Here his regiment, the Gordon Highlanders, had successfully taken the Heights of Dargai from enemy tribesmen in just forty minutes.

The tribesmen had held three battalions of the British Army at bay for hours and inflicted heavy casualties before the Gordons and Gurkhas were ordered to take the Heights. When the Gurkhas faltered, the Gordons' colonel roared: 'The General says the hill must be taken at all costs. The Gordon Highlanders WILL take it.' Under fire, the Gordons charged across 150m of open country, led by their officers and pipers. Piper Findlater was shot through both feet but propped himself up and continued playing the regimental march 'Cock o' the North' to spur on the Highlanders. They stormed up the 200m cliffs, where the shocked and intimidated tribesmen fell back. The Gordons then volunteered to carry the British Army casualties down the precipitous cliff path to safety.

The bravery of both Piper Findlater and the Gordons captured the public's imagination. On their return to Britain, the Gordon Highlanders were given a hero's welcome wherever they went.

15 August

On this day the Aberdeen Football Club we know today played its first match, holding Stenhousemuir to a 1–1 draw. Founded four months previously, the new club was an amalgamation of three existing teams: Orion ('the Stripes') who played at Cattofield, Victoria United ('the Blues') who played at Central Park and the previous Aberdeen FC ('the Whites') who played at Pittodrie. In 1899, the ground at Pittodrie had been levelled and a terrace built at the east end. Previously it had been a dunghill for police horses – the name actually means 'place of manure'.

In their first season the new Aberdeen FC played in the Northern League which covered the area south from Aberdeen to Fife. They finished only third in the league but won the Aberdeenshire Cup, which fuelled their ambition to enter the First Division of the Scottish League. At this time there was no formal promotion or relegation; the top twelve teams in the First Division voted on whether they would retain both of the existing bottom teams or would admit the top teams from the Second Division.

In 1904 Aberdeen FC was elected to the Scottish League Second Division. They signed three seasoned professionals, one from Arsenal and two from Middlesbrough, at a total cost of £210. The following season the First Division was extended to sixteen teams. One of the sixteen was Aberdeen FC.

27 September

Celebrations for the 400th anniversary of the university were delayed from 1895 until this day, when King Edward VII and Queen Alexandra opened the new Marischal College buildings. Festivities included receptions, honorary degree graduations, banquets and a ball. Lord Strathcona, university chancellor, hosted an extremely lavish banquet in a huge temporary hall constructed on neighbouring vacant land. The hall itself, designed by Alexander Marshall Mackenzie, the architect of the new buildings, could seat 4,740 people and cost £3,400. The price for the seven-course legendary 'gigantic feast' is not known.

The new buildings were even more costly than the celebrations. Purchase and demolition of the houses in front of the college alone required £75,000. A grant from the Treasury and gifts from Lord Strathcona, Charles Mitchell and his son were not sufficient and Charles Mitchell Junior eventually guaranteed the remaining amount. Marshall Mackenzie was responsible for extending the existing college, much of which had been designed by Archibald Simpson. The tower was raised and a great hall created, both named in honour of the Mitchell family. The façade was last to be completed. With its soaring granite pinnacles, this frontage on Broad Street attracted visitors from throughout Scotland in the years before the First World War. This has become the iconic view of the world's second largest granite building, most of it now leased to Aberdeen City Council for their headquarters.

3 December

At 7.30 p.m. on this evening, the orchestra struck up and the curtain was raised for *Red Riding Hood*, the first ever production at His Majesty's Theatre. All reserved seats had sold out quickly; patrons in the dress circle and orchestra stalls wore full evening dress. Police were called to control the huge crowd which queued for unreserved seats. Despite the opening performance running for four hours, the audience gave it three curtain calls.

Renowned theatre architect Frank Matcham had recently overseen the reconstruction of another Aberdeen theatre, the Tivoli, and was appointed by its owner to design his new theatre. Matcham's design reflected the new Edwardian style and was as practical as it was beautiful. Great care was taken to ensure excellent acoustics and perfect sightlines. When the Tivoli was sold two days before the opening of His Majesty's, it was with the stipulation that it should become a variety house and stage neither plays nor pantomimes.

His Majesty's Theatre flourished. Bought in the 1930s by James Donald, it was refurbished to be both theatre and cinema. The Donald family, who dominated entertainment in Aberdeen for decades, continued to manage the theatre even after the city council took over ownership. Now operated by Aberdeen Performing Arts and refurbished and extended to modern standards, it is on the 'number one UK touring circuit', often enjoying performances fresh from London's West End.

9 December

This was the day when a public sale in Turriff Market Square turned into a riot. The Scottish Insurance Commissioners, on behalf of the Chancellor of the Exchequer, attempted to sell a cow impounded from local farmer Robert Paterson.

The 1911 National Insurance Acts had been well received in towns and cities but in rural Scotland, self-reliant country folk could not see the point in paying this tax. In Aberdeenshire Robert Paterson, an upstanding member of the farming community, refused to pay on principle. By August 1913, he was due almost £4 in National Insurance for his dairy farmworkers at Lendrum near Turriff. The court fined him 15s, which he paid, but he continued to refuse to pay the tax. Sheriff Officers seized a small white Ayrshire-cross Shorthorn cow, which they undervalued at £7. At the sale and the ensuing riot, angry farmers challenged the Sheriff Officers, who were pelted with rotten fruit, eggs and soot. The cow made her escape, hotly pursued by a barking collie.

The cow was later sold privately for £7 but just a few days later was bought for £14. When the rioting farmers, including Robert Paterson, appeared in court, the case against them was found not proven. Neighbouring farmers bought the cow and led her back to Lendrum. Today, a sculpture of the cow stands in Turriff to commemorate the event.

30 July

Norwegian adventurer Tryggve Gran today took off from Cruden Bay, north of Aberdeen, and became the first person to fly across the North Sea.

Gran, the son of a Bergen shipbuilder, had travelled with a mapping expedition to the Antarctic where several geographical features are named after him. On his return journey to Norway via the USA, Gran met a pilot called Robert Lorrain and was inspired to fly across the North Sea, although he had never piloted an aircraft. After some flying hours in Britain and France, he bought a suitable aircraft from French flight pioneer Louis Blériot. With the aircraft, a Blériot XI-2 monoplane, renamed *Nordsjøen* – Norwegian for the North Sea – he travelled north to Cruden Bay. His runway here was the golden beach where, nearly 1,000 years before, a bloody battle had raged between the Scots and invading Vikings. In poor weather, Gran achieved the 320-mile crossing of the North Sea in four hours ten minutes, landing in Jæren, where Sola Airport now serves Stavanger. There was little celebration at this time due to the outbreak of the First World War just days later. There are now memorial stones at both Cruden Bay and Stavanger Sola Airport commemorating Gran's outstanding feat. On 30 July 2014, two Norwegian microlight pilots flew from Cruden Bay to Jæren to commemorate the centenary of Gran's pioneering flight.

29 August

In Aberdeen Bay on this day Prince Albert, later King George VI, was transferred by crane, in a military cot, from the hospital ship *Rohilla* onto a smaller vessel to be taken ashore. The *Rohilla* was too large to enter Aberdeen Harbour.

Prince Albert, 'Bertie', had been serving as a midshipman on board HMS *Collingwood* when he became ill with abdominal pain. His father, King George V, was alarmed by the diagnosis of appendicitis and sent three letters and three telegrams to Sir James Reid, asking him to travel to Wick to meet the ill prince. Sir James had been Queen Victoria's personal physician in Scotland and had continued to serve the royal family but was now retired. Despite this, he travelled north to sail with the prince to Aberdeen.

Sir John Marnoch, Professor of Surgery in Aberdeen, later removed the prince's inflamed appendix at an Aberdeen nursing home. Sir James Reid was asked to send a telegram to the king as soon as the operation was over and to 'telegraph twice a day for the first few days at least'. While recuperating in the nursing home, the prince was visited by his brother, later King Edward VIII, and his sister, Princess Mary. The future king made a good recovery, returned to his duties on HMS *Collingwood*, and took part in the Battle of Jutland in May 1916.

15 October

In the early weeks of the First World War, the Royal Navy believed the main risk to British shipping was from enemy surface ships on the seas between England and Europe. That view changed dramatically on this day, when a torpedo from the German submarine *U-9* struck HMS *Hawke* off the coast of Aberdeenshire.

The torpedo hit HMS *Hawke*, an Edgar-class protected cruiser, just above the engine room, where fuel caught fire and caused a large explosion. The ship immediately started taking water and sank so quickly that only seventy men survived, having managed to escape and board two lifeboats. The remaining 524 officers and men were all lost. Three of those killed were from Aberdeen, while around another twenty came from other parts of Scotland. The destroyer HMS *Swift* picked up some of the survivors while others were rescued by a Norwegian steamer, transferred to the Aberdeen steam trawler *Ben Rinnes* and returned to shore. This sinking shook Britain's press, politicians and citizens to the core. In Aberdeen, the loss of the cruiser and so many lives in local waters made people realise that the war was not only in far-away Belgium and France, but right on the city's doorstep.

25 September

This day marked a futile but costly battle in Belgium. During the days which followed, families in Aberdeen and Aberdeenshire learned of the loss in action of sons, brothers and fathers. The 4th Battalion Gordon Highlanders, including U Company, had sustained heavy casualties during the battle.

U (University) Company was a territorial unit of the Gordon Highlanders. Possibly the best-educated unit in the British Army when war was declared, the company comprised students, graduates and teaching staff of Aberdeen University. By this time, after six months in the trenches, almost all had already been wounded at least once. They went 'over the top' with the 4th Battalion at dawn on this September day to capture an enemy field gun at Hooge. This attack was intended to divert the enemy's defences from the main battle at Loos. Field Marshal Lord Kitchener, addressing the battalion beforehand, had made it clear that they and their action would be a sacrifice to ensure the success of the Loos battle. Three battalions launched the attack and U Company succeeded in taking their target, but the enemy later recaptured it. No ground was gained by the Hooge offensive. The battle left few men uninjured. Most had been killed.

U Company had left Aberdeen in November 1914. By this day in September 1915, all were seriously wounded, missing in action, or had been killed.

22 February

A mass meeting of fishermen today agreed an embargo on German trawlers' catches at Aberdeen Fishmarket. The following day, local boats remained in harbour; salesmen and fishmarket porters boycotted the foreign fish. Despite Aberdeen fish-merchants' willingness to buy the additional fish, the German vessels eventually left, their catches unsold. The dispute escalated and in early April German trawlers were stoned as they sailed into the harbour, their wheelhouse windows smashed by Aberdeen fishermen. In May an agreement was finally reached, reluctantly accepted by both fishermen and buyers, limiting the number of foreign vessels permitted to land fish in Aberdeen. Two issues had caused the dispute: low prices in Germany coupled with high prices in Aberdeen, particularly when fish was scarce; and the Germans' willingness – and Aberdeen fishermen's reluctance – to fish Icelandic waters to provide the quantity and types of fish required by Aberdeen fish-merchants.

Aberdeen had long been a seasonally-successful herring port but was otherwise an unimportant fishing centre until 1882, when steam trawling was introduced. By 1911 more than two-thirds of Scotland's 320 trawlers were registered in Aberdeen. Later, motor trawlers took over from steam and fishing became the city's most important industry. Record catches were landed at Aberdeen Fishmarket in the 1960s and '70s. The industry supported not only jobs at sea but also in buying, selling, processing and transporting fish, and in ship-building and repair yards.

2 June

An open-air swimming pool was opened on this day in Stonehaven, 15 miles south of Aberdeen. Following a poll of Stonehaven householders, it was built to the competition standard of the time: the pool is 55 yards long – just a whisker over 50m – and cost £9,529. It was filled and emptied every few days with unheated water from the nearby North Sea. Filling took less than three hours. At the opening, local children sat around the edge, their legs dangling over the side, watching as the water rushed in. The opening ceremony featured demonstrations of swimming and diving, races, parades of 'Windsor Water Woollies' including 'Riviera and Sun-Bathing Models', and a display by the 'Ladies' League of Health and Beauty', brought especially from Edinburgh for the event. There were galas throughout the season, which lasted from June until the end of September. Water polo, swimming, diving and lifesaving were taught by the pool superintendent. By the following summer a basic heating, filtration and disinfection system had been installed. During the Second World War the pool remained open and provided both recreation and showers for locally based troops.

Today the pool still opens each summer and can take up to two weeks to fill, on the rising tide, with seawater which is heated to a balmy 29°C. It is the only Olympic-size, heated seawater, art deco pool in the UK.

28 July

Today Viscount Arbuthnott officially opened Aberdeen Airport, which had been established at Dyce by air pioneer Eric Gander Dower. There was a RAF flying display, aerobatics, a 'sensational' parachute descent and a chance to 'inspect the Aeroplanes at close quarters'. Gander Dower operated flights to Glasgow, Edinburgh, northern Scotland, Orkney and Shetland and experimented with routes across the North Sea to Norway. However, the first commercial route to Norway operated from Newcastle, due to lack of radio facilities at Dyce.

During the war the airport was an important RAF base, mainly for photographic reconnaissance aircraft and, during the Battle of Britain, also fighters. A decoy airfield in the nearby countryside, lit up at night, succeeded in diverting attacks away from the airbase itself. In 1943, a Luftwaffe crew defected, landing their Junkers 88 night-fighter at Dyce. Both crew and aircraft, fitted with the latest radar equipment, provided excellent information for Allied intelligence.

In 1947 the airport was nationalised and development followed. Twenty years later, the first helicopter flew from Aberdeen to an offshore installation. The airport has expanded rapidly since that time, adding a new main passenger terminal in the 1970s and, more recently, twenty-four-hour operation and a runway extension. Scheduled and charter routes support the oil and gas industry and offer a choice of holiday destinations. It is acknowledged as the world's busiest civilian heliport.

23 September

In 1920, Professor Matthew Hay had described to the Medico-Chirugical Society his vision for co-ordinating the Aberdeen hospitals and the university's clinical departments on a shared site. At this time, well before the establishment of the National Health Service, it was necessary to raise funds from the public for such a project. The people of the north-east rose to the occasion. Many made large donations, which included gifts from landowners, bequests from retired surgeons and £1,000 from Aberdeen students. There were bazaars and house-to-house collections in the city and throughout the north-east. Tiny Fordoun in the Mearns sent over £40 from one collection. Under the leadership of Lord Provost Sir Andrew Lewis, £410,000 was raised in just two years. Later, Lord Provost Watt launched a successful appeal for 'The Last Hundred Thousand'.

On this clear sunny day, the Duke of York opened the doors to the new Aberdeen Royal Infirmary with a gold key. King Edward VIII had laid the foundation stone in 1928 while still Prince of Wales. It was intended that he would open the new hospital. However, in the throes of the controversial affair with Wallis Simpson, he delegated the duty to his younger brother who read out a message from the king during the opening ceremony. Less than three months later, the king abdicated and the Duke of York became King George VI.

10 October

This day saw the presentation of a special Short Stirling bomber aircraft to XV Squadron, Royal Air Force. During the simple ceremony, a letter from Lady MacRobert was read aloud.

When self-made millionaire Alexander MacRobert was made a baronet in 1922, his young American wife became Lady MacRobert. On his death later that year, the eldest of their three sons, Alasdair, inherited the title. He died in a civilian flying accident in 1938 and in 1941 his two younger brothers, both RAF pilots, were killed in combat within six weeks of each other. Their mother's response to their loss was to purchase aircraft for the RAF: the bomber and, later, four Hurricane fighters. Three of these aircraft were named in honour of her sons; the fourth was 'MacRobert's salute to Russia'. Contrary to popular Aberdeen myth, the Stirling bomber was not named MacRobert's Revenge but, with typical Lady MacRobert under-statement, 'MacRobert's Reply'.

On Lady MacRobert's death the family home at Tarland, 30 miles west of Aberdeen, became a care home for retired armed forces personnel. It is now a luxury country house hotel. The MacRobert Trust has contributed considerable sums of money to deserving projects throughout Scotland and particu-larly in Aberdeen. These include the restoration of Wrights and Coopers Place and Grants Place in Old Aberdeen, where a lovely memorial was also created to the MacRobert family.

18 July

Aberdeen's Lord Provost, Sir Thomas Mitchell, on this day visited the city's own warship, HMS *Scylla*, presenting gifts which included a Bible from the Sunday school children of the West Church of St Nicholas in the warship's 'mother city'.

When challenged to raise £2,750,000 during National Warship Week, from 28 February to 7 March 1942, Aberdonians met their target by the fifth day and at the end of the week the fund stood at £3,378,000. The funds for new ships came from individuals investing in War Saving schemes as part of Britain's war effort.

The money raised in Aberdeen paid for a warship already under construction and nearing completion in Greenock, the DIDO-class light cruiser HMS *Scylla*, specially armed with anti-aircraft guns. In 1942 and 1943 she was in action on Russian convoy duty and was part of the covering force for the attacks on Algiers and Sicily. In 1944, during the Normandy landings, she was the flagship of the Naval Commander Eastern Task Force when she was seriously damaged by a mine and had to withdraw to Portsmouth. She became a reserve ship after the war and was sold for breaking up in 1950.

When Leander-class destroyer HMS *Scylla* was commissioned in 1970, Aberdeen built strong connections with this new ship, culminating in 1992 when the ship's company was granted the Freedom of Aberdeen in advance of her decommissioning.

21 April

For many Aberdonians, this was the most terrifying night of the Second World War. Without warning, ten Luftwaffe bombers came in low over the city at intervals of around a minute. A second wave of fifteen aircraft flew over at around 6,000ft. This raid specifically targeted residential areas of Aberdeen, which Hitler had decreed should be bombed in revenge for the sustained bombing of Berlin by British and Russian aircraft. Within three-quarters of an hour an elite Luftwaffe squadron had dropped 130 incendiary, cluster and high-explosive bombs on Aberdeen. Many streets were left ablaze and entire families were killed. Minutes before, children had been playing in the streets. Young lads returning from a Boys' Brigade display were strafed by enemy machine-gun fire. In this one night in Aberdeen, ninety-seven civilians and twenty-seven soldiers were killed, ninety-three people were seriously wounded and a further 142 suffered minor injuries. Schools, barracks, churches and railway lines were hit and 9,000 homes were badly damaged.

As the nearest landfall for aircraft crossing the North Sea from Nazi-occupied Norway, Aberdeen had suffered many bombing raids. Built almost entirely of granite, which sparkled on moonlit and bright starry nights, the city was an easy target compared to the complete blackout in towns with soot-darkened stone. This was the last and by far the worst wartime bombing raid Aberdeen's citizens were to suffer.

14 January

The fishing boat *Girl Jean* was towed into Aberdeen Harbour on this day following a full-scale, costly three-day search involving local fishermen, RAF aircraft, the Royal Navy and Norwegian coastguard.

Four days previously, the 50ft vessel had disappeared overnight from Arbroath Harbour in Angus, south of Aberdeen. The same day, 14-year-old John Guthrie had also gone missing from his Arbroath home. During the war young John had spent a lot of time speaking to the Norwegian seamen based at the harbour, watching and learning seafaring skills from them. He had once been found 70 miles offshore, stowed away on the *Girl Jean*, and it seemed likely he had now stolen the boat to sail to Norway. With fuel to travel 500 miles and no crew aboard except the teenager, the boat's owners, the authorities and the Guthrie family feared the worst. Late on 13 January, however, the Hull trawler *Reptonian* had found the boat in heavy seas between the Scottish coast and Norway. Crewmen risked their lives jumping from the trawler onto *Girl Jean*. They found the boy, seasick and shivering, in the fish hold.

In Aberdeen the crowd cheered and seamen marvelled at his skill but John lived to regret his actions. Sentenced by a juvenile court to three-and-a-half years at an 'approved school', he also lost the opportunity for his dream career in the Royal Navy.

31 October

Aberdeen's Mither Kirk had been one of the largest medieval burgh kirks in Scotland. It was divided after the Reformation and, by the mid-1800s, both West and East churches had been restored. The East church was lit by magnificent gas chandeliers, called 'sunlights'. In 1874 a fire started in a sunlight and spread rapidly along roof timbers to the ancient oak steeple which connected the churches. Within twenty minutes, the 43m-high spire had fallen. The bells inside, said to be the finest peal in Scotland, were ruined. Their scrap value was used as part-payment for a new peal of bells. These were rung for the first time at Queen Victoria's Golden Jubilee in 1887 but were found to be defective in design and tuning.

These bells were recast, new ones were added and all were accurately tuned. On this morning, a service of dedication was held for the Mither kirk's new bells. 'The Bourdon', the largest, weighs 4½ tons. A further thirty-six comprised a carillon. During the dedication, the Doxology was played on the bells and, over the next three days, the carillonneur played nine recitals of classical, religious and popular music. The carillon framework had been planned to house additional bells and, two years later, eleven new ones were added to give St Nicholas church a full forty-eight-bell carillon. Today, music played on the carillon sounds absolutely magnificent.

12 May

Aberdeen's first tram rails had been laid in the summer of 1874. Horse-drawn trams provided transport to Queen's Cross and Causewayend. Other services were quickly added, including routes from Holburn Junction to Mannofield and Kittybrewster to Woodside. In 1901 an electric tram started running from Castlegate to the Bathing Station.

By the late 1950s many cities were replacing their trams. Buses offered more route flexibility and were also more comfortable for passengers. By March 1958, only 'the Bridges' tramline remained in Aberdeen. Thousands watched the ceremonial final six-vehicle tram journey, led by a horse-drawn tram.

A report to the Council's Transport Committee advised that the first tram to be broken up for scrap had realised only £85 net of dismantling costs. The Committee therefore agreed to accept an offer for the remaining forty-two tramcars from Bird's Commercial Motors Ltd of Stratford-on-Avon. Their bid was the highest: £5,400, or £128 per tram. However, Bird's preferred method of dismantling tramcars was rather unconventional and special permission was required. Finally, on this night, the remaining forty-two trams were burned on the private tramway track at the Queen's Links near the beach. Only one week later, Tommy Bird and his work squad had reduced the burned-out remains to 500 tons of scrap metal. They had also cleared twenty lorry-loads of ashes and scrap from Beach Boulevard, where the trams had been broken up.

24 July

This was the day when 17-year-old Aberdonian Ian Black stood on the podium to receive his gold medal at the British Empire and Commonwealth Games in Cardiff. He had qualified for the 220 yards butterfly final by winning his heat and swam the final in 2 minutes 22.6 seconds, almost 3 seconds clear of the silver medallist. He also won two silver medals in freestyle events at these Games. Later this summer he broke five European records and took three gold medals for Great Britain in the European Championships in Budapest, winning not only butterfly but also both 400m and 1500m freestyle. Towards the end of the year, Ian was voted winner of BBC Sports Review of the Year, the youngest person, and first Scot, to win the award. At the Rome Olympics in 1960, in the days before accurate timing, he swam the 400m freestyle in exactly the same time as the bronze medal winner, but was judged to be fourth.

After working in education in Scotland, Canada and Hong Kong, Ian Black returned to Aberdeen as Head of Robert Gordon's College Junior School, which he had attended as a pupil. This is a school with a tradition for swimming excellence dating from 1870, which also produced Olympic, Commonwealth and European medallist Neil Cochran and, during Ian's time on the staff, Commonwealth Games Gold medallist David Carry.

15 August

Today, Henry John Burnett was hanged at Craiginches Prison, Aberdeen. This was the last execution in Scotland. Outside the prison, crowds of Aberdonian men, women and children had gathered. The death penalty was suspended the following year and banned permanently in 1969.

Henry Burnett and Margaret Guyan had met and fallen in love at the fish factory where they worked. At 23, she was two years older and already married. She left her husband and, with her sons, moved in with 'Harry'. She soon discovered he had a violent temper and flew into rages when he would lock her in their city-centre flat. On 31 May, she left him and went to her grandmother's house where she met her estranged husband, Tom. Burnett meantime stole his brother's double-barrelled shotgun and arrived at the house. There, in Margaret's presence, he shot Tom Guyan in the head. The couple hijacked a car and went on the run. Margaret even agreed to marry him but they were soon tracked down and he was arrested. Less than three months later, following a trial when he pled insanity – which he later refuted in a letter to Margaret – he was executed and buried within the prison grounds. In January 2014, with the prison due to close, his family agreed to the exhumation and cremation of his body. The prison was demolished in 2015.

1964

21 May

This was a fateful day for Aberdeen, when the city's Medical Officer of Health confirmed that twenty-one people were in hospital with typhoid fever. At this time Aberdeen was a thriving holiday destination but the 1964 season was cut short by Scotland's worst ever typhoid outbreak.

The source of the disease was a catering tin of corned beef, poorly sealed and contaminated by untreated cooling water at the processing factory in Argentina and sold unwittingly by an Aberdeen grocer. Bacteria from the infected meat spread to other foods on knives, hands and the slicing machine. The disease spread rapidly and, with little initial understanding of how the infection passed from person to person, Aberdonians were afraid. Once they learned that good hygiene was the key to preventing infection, the epidemic was halted. By then, 469 cases had been confirmed. Fortunately there were no fatalities.

For many, the epidemic was life changing. Infected adults and children were quarantined in hospital for up to three months, their only contact with relatives and friends through locked windows. Schools were closed, social events were cancelled, few outsiders ventured into the city and Aberdonians were ostracised if they travelled. For some, medication continued for months, affecting studies and employment. Tourism businesses folded and jobs were lost. Only when the queen visited were people reassured that it was safe to come to Aberdeen again.

1 November

Around 1.15 p.m. on this day a building under construction collapsed in high winds. This was to have been the university's new zoology building in Old Aberdeen. It was designed as a steel and concrete interpretation of the façade of Marischal College. Eyewitnesses described a huge roar and the building going down 'like a pack of cards'.

Eight men were buried under hundreds of tons of steel and rubble. The sheer size of the seven-storey building hindered initial rescue attempts. It had been over 25m high, 65m long and 13m wide. Fire-fighters joined construction-site workmen, some of whom were tearing at lumps of concrete with their bare hands. Eventually, three injured men were rescued. Two joiners, two steel-erectors and a builder's labourer died in the wrecked building. The last of the five bodies was finally recovered seventeen hours after the collapse. The Lord Provost called this a week of disaster for the city, as three Aberdeen headmistresses and a primary school supervisor had died in a fire in Stornoway a few days previously.

The Fatal Accident Enquiry into the building collapse determined that, with no wind-resisting connections, the steel structure had been in an unstable condition. This is believed to have been the first total progressive collapse of a steel structure anywhere in the world. Three years later, the university's new zoology building, safely constructed, finally opened.

2 December

Hundreds of people queued outside the High Court in Aberdeen from the early hours of this morning to hear the verdict returned on Alan Peters, Brian Tevendale and Sheila Garvie, who were accused of murdering Sheila's husband Maxwell on the night of 14/15 May.

Sheila had reported her husband missing from their farmhouse in the Mearns countryside, south of Aberdeen, in May. His body was found in a disused quarry three months later, after Sheila had confessed to her mother, who informed the police. Maxwell had been shot in the head. Sheila, her young lover Brian Tevendale and Alan Peters were arrested. Sheila and Tevendale each blamed the other for Maxwell's death and implicated Peters, who had accompanied Tevendale on the fateful night.

The trial caused a sensation. Even in the 'swinging sixties', many people around the country were shocked by Sheila Garvie's defence motion regarding her husband's 'unnatural and perverted sexual practices', the evidence of his affairs with men and women, and watching her having sex with Tevendale. Tales of the foursomes in which the Garvies, Tevendale and his married sister participated had become the subject of gossip in the Mearns. The base for Maxwell's 'nudist club', deep in the Aberdeenshire countryside near Alford (pronounced 'áfford'), became known as 'Kinky Cottage'.

Tavendale and Garvie were sentenced to life imprisonment for the murder. The charge against Peters was found not proven.

2 February

On this day, Aberdonians learned their city had been excluded from the national 'Britain in Bloom' competition to allow other cities an opportunity for success. Having first won in 1965, Aberdeen had then taken the trophy in 1969, 1970 and 1971. Despite repeated exclusions, the city has won the national award eleven times, most recently in 2006, and the Gold City award in 2014. In 1989, Aberdeen was given outright the trophy for Best Scottish City after winning it annually from 1968, then went on to win the new trophy a further twenty-one times.

Much of Aberdeen's floral heritage is due to the vision and innovation of David Welch, Director of Parks for twenty-five years. In 1968 the council agreed with his suggestion that roses should replace grass in the ring road's central reservation, earning him the nickname 'Mr Roses'. Grass, he argued, required weekly cutting while roses needed only infrequent pruning. Throughout the 1970s, he encouraged schools and youth groups to raise funds by sponsored bulb-plantings rather than sponsored walks. The children learned from their experience, watched the flowers bloom and grew up proud and protective of 'their' flowers. Each spring, around 42 million crocuses and daffodils bloom in public spaces, parks and gardens. All summer, hanging baskets and window boxes enhance the city centre. Year-round, the David Welch Winter Gardens in Duthie Park are a colourful, fragrant oasis.

13 August

The Athenaeum had been purpose-designed by Archibald Simpson as a high-ceilinged, light reading room for Aberdeen citizens. It was later converted to a hotel, restaurant and grill room and became the Royal Athenaeum after a Warrant was granted by King George V. Aberdonians called it 'Jimmie Hays' after its owner, even after it changed hands in 1965.

Late on this night, staff reported a fire to a passing policeman. The fire spread rapidly behind false ceilings and floors; by a few minutes after midnight, flames were shooting through the roof. Despite firemen having withdrawn repeatedly for their own safety, the fire was under control by 2.25 a.m. Twelve fire engines attended, some from as far as Stonehaven and Kintore; Inverurie engines were also on standby. A police constable, treated for smoke inhalation at Woolmanhill, was the only casualty. Four floors of the building were destroyed and tons of rubble from the roof threatened to crash through to the ground floor, itself already damaged by smoke and water. The east wall was standing 'almost free'. The Firemaster's initial investigation indicated a dropped cigarette end had probably ignited upholstery.

Later, the building was restored as the Royal Athenaeum pub-restaurant with offices above. The upper floors, refurbished to a high standard, are now suites for a nearby hotel and the ground floor and basement have been developed by local craft brewers to create a bar and club.

3 November

At 12.40 p.m. today, Queen Elizabeth pressed a symbolic button at BP's Dyce headquarters to start the flow of Britain's first oil. The control console suddenly came to life, showing the oil being pumped by undersea pipeline from the Forties Field deep below the North Sea to Cruden Bay, then underground for its 127-mile journey to Grangemouth.

Almost exactly five years previously, BP had announced they had struck oil 110 miles east of Aberdeen. Drilling on one block had shown slight traces of oil which was unlikely to be commercial. The neighbouring block was more promising and, drilling the third, the crew had to abandon the well and take to the lifeboats after hitting surface gas. Gas is extremely dangerous, powering itself and accelerating at 1,000 feet per second. It is also an indication that oil may be present.

With a fast-changing situation in the Middle East, which at this time supplied most of the UK's oil, the government encouraged BP to produce the oil as soon as possible. Four production platforms, each tall enough to withstand the North Sea's worst weather, were designed by BP engineers. Each cost £400 million and produced oil from thirty-six wells, 100m below the surface of the sea. Forties production was expected to save the country £250,000 in imported oil every day. It had cost BP £745 million to explore and evaluate the Forties Field.

28 August

This was the day when the world's first full-body Magnetic Resonance Imaging (MRI) scan was conducted in Aberdeen. The patient, from Fraserburgh, was terminally ill with cancer. A team led by the University of Aberdeen's Professor of Medical Physics, John Mallard, had built the scanner.

MRI works by placing a patient – or part of a patient – inside a strong magnetic field. The scanner uses hydrogen atoms in the water molecules within human tissue to provide a signal to create a 3D image. This shows any irregularities, such as tumours and soft tissue injuries. Now used throughout the world, it can see inside the body without the need for invasive surgery. It has become a powerful diagnostic and research tool for a wide range of diseases and conditions including cancer, multiple sclerosis, dementia, brain tumours, strokes and sports injuries.

Professor Mallard also played a crucial role in the development of Nuclear Medicine Imaging, which includes Positron Emission Tomography (PET). As early as the 1960s, he predicted that PET would become one of the most powerful tools for studying human diseases. The clinical benefits of PET imaging are now widely recognised in the management and treatment of cancer and other conditions. Professor Mallard was instrumental in bringing Scotland's first PET scanner to Aberdeen. A new state-of-the-art PET scanner was launched by one of his students, Professor Peter Sharp, in January 2015.

11 May

Their crushing defeat of Rangers in the 1982 Scottish Cup entitled Aberdeen Football Club, known as 'the Dons', to take part in the European Cup Winners' Cup, now replaced by the UEFA Cup. The team had played well in the early rounds, beating the Swiss, Albanian and Polish Cup winners, and had excelled themselves in the quarter-finals, winning against mighty Bayern Munich. Following a resounding semi-final victory for the Dons against Belgium's Waterschei Thor, the city held its breath.

The final against Real Madrid was held in Gothenburg, Sweden, on this day. Aberdeen became football-mad; even Aberdonians who were not usually interested in football were desperate to attend. Tickets for special direct flights to Gothenburg sold almost instantly. The Shetland ferry of the time, MV *St Clair*, was chartered and sailed to Gothenburg with 500 fans. At the Ullevi Stadium the rain sheeted down as Aberdeen scored the first goal, followed by an equaliser from Real Madrid. However, after extra time the score was 2-1 in favour of the Dons.

The city went wild with excitement and gave a rapturous welcome not only to the team and their manager, Alex Ferguson, but also to the returning fans, who had behaved impeccably. Later in 1983, Aberdeen won the European Super Cup against Hamburg, but it is this day, and the Gothenburg victory, which Aberdonians best remember and savour.

25 October

On this Tuesday, just before 9 a.m., a large explosion shattered the normally peaceful Aberdeen suburb of Cults. The blast centred on the four-star Royal Darroch Hotel and thoughts turned to terrorism. However, it was gas, not a bomb, which had ripped the hotel apart. The roof and front of the building were blown off. Glass from shattered windows damaged passing vehicles. The ground floor collapsed into the basement and fire spread rapidly through the ruined building. Within four minutes, the first fire engines arrived. Aberdeen Royal Infirmary's disaster plan was implemented. Four members of hotel staff and two guests lost their lives and many more were injured.

On the fateful morning, workers were repairing an underground gas leak near the hotel when a falling brick severed a vulnerable impulse pipe. Gas pressure in the local area rose dramatically. The hotel's gas meters parted at the seams and an explosive mixture of natural gas and air filled the basement. The Fatal Accident Enquiry later found that the explosion could have been prevented had meter governors been fitted in the hotel. Scottish Gas had been aware of the lack of these governors for six months but had done nothing to rectify this. They admitted liability and invited claims from people injured or bereaved by the explosion.

6 July

The sound of helicopters awakened Aberdonians during this night, as the injured from the world's worst offshore oil disaster were flown to Aberdeen Royal Infirmary's helipad.

A few hours previously, 120 miles north-east of Aberdeen, the Piper Alpha Platform had exploded when gas escaped from a pump's pressure safety valve which had been stripped for maintenance. Despite clear instructions not to use this pump, this information had not reached the relevant people. When the working pump failed, the disabled pump was switched on, causing the initial huge blast. Within a short time, gas from other fields, being piped to the mainland via Piper Alpha, caused a second massive explosion. Rescue helicopters were beaten back by dense smoke, toxic fumes and raging flames. Some men escaped from the blazing platform by dropping to the sea 30m below, although the surface of the sea was also ablaze with burning oil. Survivors were picked up by standby-safety vessels *Silver Pit* and *Sandhaven*. Many men were trapped inside the burning platform as it collapsed beneath the waves. Of the 226 men on board Piper Alpha this night, 165 perished. Two crew from the *Sandhaven* also died. Later, seven crewmen from the two standby-safety vessels were awarded the George Medal for acts of great bravery. On boarding the wrecked platform, the legendary oil well firefighter Red Adair said, 'it's the worst thing I've ever seen.'

DEDICATED TO
THE MEMORY OF THE
ONE HUNDRED AND SIXTY SEVEN MEN
WHO LOST THEIR LIVES
IN THE
PIPER ALPHA OIL PLATFORM DISASTER

8TH JULY 1988

25 June

By early 1989 the oil and gas industry already had its own inter-denominational chaplaincy but no dedicated chapel. The most appropriate place for an 'oil chapel' was within the Kirk of St Nicholas, Aberdeen's Mither Kirk, the church at the heart of the settlement which grew up around the harbour.

In medieval times there had been an altar to St John in the north transept. St John is the patron saint of oilmen and this ancient place of worship was chosen to become the oil chapel. Refurbished by the industry to mark the first quarter century of North Sea operations, it was dedicated on this day in the presence of the Princess Royal.

A stunningly beautiful stained-glass window, created by Scottish artist Sheena McInnes, draws you into the tranquillity of the chapel. The symbolic window vividly depicts Aberdeen's two rivers, the Dee and the Don, as they flow from Aberdeenshire's grain-producing hinterland past the city's historic buildings to the sea. In the North Sea is a fishing boat with its catch and oil installations, pipelines and platform support vessels. Other furnishings include a tapestry and chairs, a table and screen crafted by Tim Stead from a range of symbolic woods. A new Book of Remembrance, dedicated in July 2013 on the twenty-fifth anniversary of the Piper Alpha tragedy, commemorates all who have died offshore since then.

8 August

From 10.30 a.m. on this sunny Thursday morning, the vessels taking part in the Cutty Sark Tall Ships' Race left the harbour for their Parade of Sail in Aberdeen Bay before competing in the last stage of the race.

The ships had been berthed at quaysides in the heart of the city centre. Some had come from the Continent. Others had sailed from Belfast, with the smaller vessels passing through the Caledonian Canal and the larger braving the Pentland Firth between mainland Scotland and the Orkney Islands.

Thousands of locals thronged the quaysides to visit the vessels and enjoy five days of festivities. There were fun inter-crew competitions, street markets, a Bavarian beer festival celebrating Aberdeen's long-standing twinning with Regensburg, and Aberdeen Football Club played Manchester United. Each day the Household Cavalry marched and performed a musical ride. The Gordon Highlanders' Band Beat the Retreat on the quayside each evening. On the final morning, spectator flights by slow, vintage 'Dakota' aircraft provided magnificent leisurely views of the Parade of Sail. The Parade concluded with a display by much faster aircraft – the RAF Red Arrows aerobatic display team. The captain of the Polish schooner *Zawisza Czarny* wrote: 'Aberdeen was our dream port … our happiness [was] even greater due to the hand of friendship offered by the people of Aberdeen … The image of your country will remain with us for ever …'

12 June

Robert Gordon's Hospital had become a day school, Robert Gordon's College, in 1881. Day and evening classes were introduced for adults, boys and girls to study primary, secondary and mechanical subjects. Within a few years there were more than 1,200 students who attended scientific, technical and commercial classes. Before the turn of the century, the Aberdeen Mechanics' Institute and Aberdeen Pharmaceutical Society had transferred their classes and training to the college, and Gray's School of Science and Art had been founded. Robert Gordon's original aim, to prepare sons and grandsons of Aberdeen's Baillies for trade, had not only been met but also exceeded.

In 1965, the technical college became Robert Gordon's Institute of Technology, known locally as RGIT. This change was in keeping with its founder's belief in educating Aberdonians to give them the skills and knowledge necessary for success throughout the world. It also reflected the institute's growing reputation as a centre of excellence in non-university higher education. RGIT embraced the opportunities offered by the discovery of oil and gas beneath the North Sea and Aberdeen's growing importance as an oil city.

On this day, RGIT achieved university status; once again Aberdeen had two universities. The Robert Gordon University today offers industry-led courses in degrees and awards relevant to employers. In 2014, the Higher Education Statistics Agency confirmed its position as first in the UK for graduate employment.

10 December

Since the mid-1960s, when oil companies set up their first bases at the harbour, Aberdeen's fortunes have been closely linked to the price of oil. World events, outwith the control of anyone in Aberdeen, affect supply and demand, leading to wide fluctuations in price. Many North Sea fields are difficult and costly to develop; the relationship between the price of Brent Crude and production cost is of vital importance to the city's, and Britain's, economy.

On this day, the Brent oil price fell to its lowest level in recent times, $9.10 per barrel. When the price remains low and production costs are high, exploration and evaluation stop, unnecessary expenditure is cut, projects to develop difficult fields are mothballed and redundancies become reality. The ripples reach out to affect all businesses in Aberdeen and its hinterland: hotels, shops, restaurants and bars also lay-off staff.

The highest ever price, almost $150 per barrel in early 2008, did not last but the dip was followed by several years of a sustained high price of $100–$120. At this time, Aberdeen enjoyed virtually full employment and many offices and homes were built for the influx of new workers.

Despite a downturn in late 2014, some developments continued, including the 'impossible' Mariner Field. In July 2015, BP announced a new $1 billion investment at a time when Brent Crude was trading at around $49 per barrel.

18 July

Aberdonian golfer Paul Lawrie was by this time ranked 159th in the world. He had won two major championships, the 1996 Catalonia Open and, earlier in 1999, the Qatar Masters but had to qualify to play in the 1999 British Open. On this day, the famous Claret Jug was presented to Paul after he won the Open at Carnoustie. He was the first Scotsman to win the Open on native soil for almost seventy years and the first qualifier to win since exemptions had first been introduced in 1963.

Carnoustie was close enough for Paul to travel each day from his Aberdeen home. It had not hosted the Open since 1975 and its return in 1999 was controversial. On the final day Paul was ten strokes behind but stormed through the final round to win a place in a four-hole play-off against Jean Van de Velde and Justin Leonard. He calmly went ahead at the third and at the fourth his second shot landed just 3ft from the hole, sealing the championship.

Paul still lives in Aberdeen and in 2015 his vision for a new European Tour event 'in his backyard' became a reality with the Saltire Energy Paul Lawrie Match Play championship at Murcar Links. The Paul Lawrie Foundation, based in Aberdeen, encourages young local golfers to play to the best of their ability and to have fun.

20 April

In 1868, a station fit for royal visitors had opened at Ballater, the terminus of the Deeside railway, close to Balmoral. It was an attractive building with a *porte cochère* to shelter royal carriages and their influential occupants. In 1896 it had been repainted in the Imperial livery of black and gold to welcome Tsar Nicholas to what was already 'Royal Deeside'.

In the 1960s, with few people using the service, the Deeside line and the station closed. In 2000, the historic building was sympathetically restored to house shops, a restaurant, visitor information centre and magnificent Victorian-themed attraction, complete with royal waiting room and Queen Victoria's toilet.

On this day, Prince Charles formally opened the Old Royal Station. He was fascinated with the Victorian displays and interpretation and regaled invited guests with his own memories of arriving at the station as a small boy, excited to see the Royal Guard drawn up to honour his mother. However, he felt the restored station lacked a train and urged the partners responsible to provide a restored royal carriage. Almost exactly seven years later, the prince opened a meticulous replica of Queen Victoria's Day Saloon which visitors could board to see how the royal party had travelled over a century before.

Sadly, the Old Royal Station was devastated by fire in May 2015 but at the time of writing is to be restored to its former glory.

21 September

Aberdeen Harbour Board today inaugurated the new Marine Operations Centre, 'the MOC', with a meeting and a visit for stakeholders. The harbour has been a trust port since 1961. This means there are no shareholders to be paid and profits are invested in improvements to benefit the harbour's stakeholders.

The MOC, completed at a cost of £3.7 million, is one of many recent investments. It was built to provide a new base for Vessel Traffic Services, previously located in The Roundhouse. This historic white tower, much loved by generations of Aberdonians, is now leased as offices. The MOC, in a prominent position where the North Pier meets the land, has also become a favourite landmark. Its award-winning design represents two elements: a stylised, traditional white lighthouse, and steel and glass echoing the bow and bridge of a ship. The light and airy glass structure reflects the surroundings and appears almost to float in front of the tower. This extremely practical building provides a base for the Port Marine Superintendent and harbour pilots and houses radar tracking equipment and a ship's bridge simulator for training and emergency response drills. Vessel Traffic Services, similar to an airport control tower, are on the top floor. This gives excellent views across the harbour and out to the Fairway Buoy, where harbour pilots board and leave the ships they guide in and out of the port.

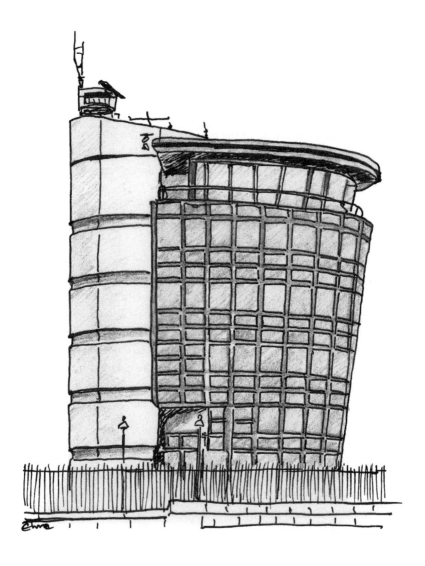

16 April

When Rubislaw Quarry closed in 1971, it was Europe's largest man-made hole. Although it is a much-loved Aberdeen 'landmark', few people have actually seen it. Hugh Black and Sandy Whyte, who bought the quarry on this day, had not seen it since they had played there as teenagers forty years before. When they asked to see their purchase, the seller advised access was by cutting a hole in the fence, which would need to be repaired afterwards.

By this time the 142m-deep hole was flooded and a boat was needed to explore the property. The water was also rising significantly and, using Aberdeen-based oil and gas industry expertise, they brought in a submersible pump to lower the water level. Oil industry sub-sea technology was also used to undertake a sub-surface survey. Neither pumping nor survey was straightforward. Initially there was no electricity on site, the original quarry drainage outlet could not be used, and – not least – the survey required an 11-tonne vessel to be lowered into the quarry by crane. Using both state-of-the-art sonar equipment and a ROV (Remotely Operated Vehicle), the survey provided exciting 2D and 3D images of what lies below the surface.

Hugh and Sandy developed plans for an innovative £6 million granite heritage centre to overlook the quarry. Despite Sandy's death in 2015, this is still scheduled to proceed and will give 'the Granite City' a well-deserved, unique attraction.

1 July

Aberdeen has long been a centre for agriculture, its citizens well used to the sights – and smells – of the countryside. Until a new mart opened in 1990, auctions were held not far from the city centre. Occasionally animals escaped and stampeding 'fine fattened' pigs held up trams on various occasions. In 1949, a stirk ran into a Castlegate shop, where the assistant calmly moved vulnerable goods from its path. In 1980, an excited bullock was cornered in the playground of Northfield Academy. Some years later, another galloped into the city centre, almost becoming 'a bull in a china shop' when it stopped at a specialist store. All these animals were recaptured and removed safely.

Cattle and sheep are transported regularly by sea to Aberdeen from Orkney and Shetland for fattening and sale. On this day a cow broke free while being loaded onto a float at Aberdeen Harbour and galloped off. Despite the best rescue attempts by lifeboat crews, the cow got into the water and swam strongly to the other side, causing temporary closure of the navigation channel. Following five hours of freedom, it became clear that the animal was becoming a threat to its rescuers and, battered against the breakwater wall by waves, it was in danger of serious injury. In the interests of animal welfare and public safety, the cow was humanely dispatched by police marksmen.

10 September

On this evening, over half a million pounds were raised for charity at an auction of dolphin sculptures.

For ten weeks during the summer of 2014, Aberdeen's streets, gardens and visitor attractions had come alive with fifty colourful dolphin sculptures. The street art project, which was inspired by the bottlenose dolphins which live year-round in the North Sea near Aberdeen's busy harbour, aimed to raise money for both Whale and Dolphin Conservation and the ARCHIE Foundation, the official charity of the Royal Aberdeen Children's Hospital.

In June, the sculptures had appeared beside important buildings, by the harbour, at the airport and train station, in parks and gardens and open spaces. Sponsored by local companies and organisations, the sculptures were designed by several local artists using paint, mosaic and even wool and willow. Inspiration came from the sea, trees, birds, space, local landmarks, and the Northern Lights. Aberdonians and visitors were captivated by the project and followed the dolphin trail, many taking 'selfies' (or 'dolphies') of themselves with the dolphins. The whole 'pod' was brought together for a final viewing weekend before the auction. Prices bid ranged from £3,000 upwards, the highest being £55,000, which was paid for 'Golfin Dolphin', based on Royal Aberdeen Golf Course and signed by all the competitors at the Scottish Open held there this summer. In total, the auction raised £531,000 for the two charities.

2015

3 July

Contractors working on pipes and cabling for a new boiler for a Schoolhill building today uncovered a human skeleton. This was no surprise. The Blackfriars, or Dominicans, were known to have occupied the site until the Protestant Reformation and the contractors had employed an archaeologist to monitor all soil stripping. What was surprising, however, was that the skeleton was only 40cm below the surface and was the first of thirty to be carefully uncovered by archaeologists.

Between 1230 and 1249, King Alexander II had founded a Dominican house and had given to it his palace and garden, situated between modern Schoolhill, Blackfriars Street, Woolmanhill, St Andrews Street and Harriet Street. The archaeologists also found the remains of a wall, possibly the east wall of the Blackfriars church. The skeletons lay to the east of this in what is thought to have been the burial ground of the Blackfriar friary. Both friary and church had been destroyed in the mid-1500s during the Reformation. The remains of men, women and children, including a very young baby, are believed to have been members of wealthy Aberdeen families. The baby, possibly newborn, was uncovered in the upper fill of an adult grave. Once the remains were lifted, work recommenced onsite. Following radiocarbon dating to establish when the burials had taken place, the remains were reburied in consecrated ground close to their original resting place. In February 2016, the remains of a further ninety-two bodies were found nearby during excavations for the renovation of Aberdeen Art Gallery.

Sources and References

BOOKS, BOOKLETS AND GUIDEBOOKS

Aberdeen's Bridges over the Dee and Don (Aberdeen City Libraries Local Studies Department)

Aberdeen *Evening Express*

Aberdeen Journal/Press and Journal

Allan, Richard Crossley, *The Landing of Queen Victoria at Aberdeen, 8th September 1848* (Aberdeen, Taylor & Henderson, Her Majesty's Printers, 1898)

Anderson, Peter John (ed.), *Charters and other writs illustrating the history of the Royal Burgh of Aberdeen, 1171–1804* (Aberdeen, New Spalding Club, 1890)

Barrett, Dom Michael, *A Calendar of Scottish Saints* (CreateSpace Independent Publishing Platform, 2014)

Barrow, G.W.S., *The Charters of King David I: The written Acts of David I King of Scots* (Boydell Press, 2008)

Bennett, P.N., Paper: *Alexander Gordon (1752-99) and his writing: insights into medical thinking in the late eighteenth century* (Edinburgh, Royal College of Physicians of Edinburgh, 2012)

Bolton, Paul, Briefing Note: *Oil Prices* (London, Library of the House of Commons, January 2014)

Brogden, W.A., *Aberdeen, An Illustrated Architectural Guide* (Edinburgh, The Rutland Press, 1998 & Edinburgh, RIAS, 2012)

Cassells, Ian, *No more Paraffin-Oilers*, (Caithness, Whittles Publishing, 2000)

Croly, Christopher P., *Torry Coastal Trail*, (Aberdeen City Council)

Croly, Christopher P., *Aberdeen's Jacobite Trail* (Aberdeen City Council)

Croly, Christopher P., *The Battle of Harlaw* (Aberdeen City Council)

Duff, David (Ed.), *Queen Victoria's Highland Journals* (London, The Reed Consumer Books Ltd for Lomond Books, 1994)

Francis, Edward, *Master Blenders, the enduring spirit of Chivas Brothers* (Whitley, Good Books (GB Publications Ltd), 1998)

Gardiner, Michael, *At the Edge of Empire: The Life of Thomas B. Glover* (Edinburgh, Birlinn Ltd, 2007)

Hibbert, Christopher, *Queen Victoria, A Personal History* (London, HarperCollins, 2000)

Jillings, K.J., *Plague, Pox and the Physician in Aberdeen, 1495–1516* (Edinburgh, Royal College of Physicians of Edinburgh, 2010)

John Fyfe, One hundred and fifty years 1846–1996 (Kemnay, Time Pieces Publications)

Mackay, Alexander, *Scottish Samurai Thomas Blake Glover 1838–1911* (Edinburgh, Canongate Press, 1997)

Marran, Peter, *Grampian Battlefields* (Aberdeen, Aberdeen University Press, 1990)

Mitchell, G.A.G., *The Book of Aberdeen; Resurrection Days* (Aberdeen, 1939, ed. David Rorie)

Morgan, Diane, *Lost Aberdeen* (Edinburgh, Birlinn Ltd, 2004)

Potter, Harry *Blood Feud: The Murrays and the Gordons at War in the Age of Mary, Queen of Scots* (The History Press, 2002)

Ritchie, George F., *The Real Price of Fish* (Beverley, Hutton Press Ltd, 1991)

Smith, Robin, *The Making of Scotland* (Edinburgh, Canongate Books Ltd, 2001)

Swan, Edi, *His Majesty's Theatre, One Hundred Years of Glorious Damnation* (Edinburgh, Black & White Publishing, 2006)

Webster, Jack *The first 100 Years of the Dons: the official history of Aberdeen Football Club 1903–2003* (London, Hodder & Stoughton, 2003)

ONLINE

www.abdn.ac.uk
www.aberdeen-angus.co.uk
www.aberdeencity.gov.uk
www.aberdeenships.com
www.anglicanhistory.org
British Library media database
www.britishnewspaperarchive.co.uk
www.canmore.rcahms.gov.uk
www.carnoustiegolflinks.co.uk
www.celebrate-scotland.co.uk/News-and-Features/1010/An_expert_guide_
    to_the_Breviary_of_Aberdeen_-_Scotlands_first_printed_book/
www.cushnieent.force9.co.uk
www.eia.gov (US Energy Information Administration)
www.forces-war-records.co.uk
www.kirk-of-st-nicholas.org.uk
www.mcjazz.f2s.com
www.med-chi.co.uk
www.mugiemoss.co.uk
www.nam.ac.uk (National Army Museum)
www.nbl.snl.no (Norsk biografisk leksikon)
www.nlb.org.uk/LighthouseLibrary/Lighthouse/Girdle-Ness/
www.paullawriegolf.com
www.royalaberdeengolf.com
www.rubislawquarry.co.uk
www.saintwiki.com

www.scotland.org
www.scottishgolfhistory.org
www.scottish-places.info (gazetteer for Scotland)
www.seventradesofaberdeen.co.uk
www.shoreporters.com
www.tea.co.uk/tea-clippers
www.theopen.com
www.ukoilandgaschaplaincy.com
www.wilddolphins.org.uk
www.xvsqnassociation.co.uk

OTHER

Aberdeen Maritime Museum permanent exhibitions
Bishop William Elphinstone exhibition, Aberdeen University, October 2014
Gordon Highlanders Museum video and exhibits

About the Author

ELMA MCMENEMY was born and brought up in Edinburgh. She graduated from Aberdeen University in 1975 and has lived in Aberdeenshire ever since. She is a professional Blue Badge Scottish Tourist Guide and tourism consultant. This is her second book for The History Press. The first was *Bloody Scottish History: Aberdeen*.

Also from The History Press

SCOTLAND

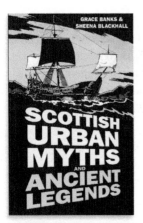

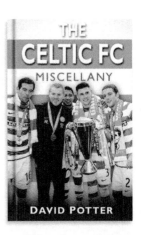

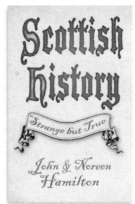

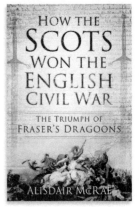